Joan moves in the miraculous and desires to see others changed through the power of Jesus Christ and the Holy Spirit. She exemplifies integrity of the highest order and has a way of drawing this quality out of others. Her heart of compassion is evident as she ministers to those in need.

—**Marilyn Hickey**
Founder and President, Marilyn Hickey Ministries

Supernatural Provision is a lifelong learning manual for financial freedom. As we operate with economic realities from a biblical perspective, we will experience the faithfulness of God to continually open the windows of heaven, pour out a blessing we don't have room enough to contain, and surprise us again and again by His grace.

—**Dr. Mark J. Chironna**
Mark Chironna Ministries
Orlando, Florida

Christians need to read this book again and again and share its valuable insights with family and friends.

—**Dr. Tom Leding**
Best-selling author
Founder, Tom Leding Ministries
International Director, FGBMFI

Every believer who applies these simple yet powerful Spirit-directed action steps will produce an abundant harvest of God's promised blessings and receive the abundance God is longing to lavish upon all of us in these last days.

—**Jeff Mendenhall**
President and CEO, Economic Destiny Institute

After a weekend with Joan and several of her team members, my wife was released from fear and launched into leading worship at our church. Now, our worship has risen to a new level.

—**Reverend Ryan M. Miller**
Senior Pastor, Greenwood Assembly of God
Fayetteville, Pennsylvania

Joan Hunter's spiritual insight brings fresh understanding that will remove hindrances and catapult you into the realm where you can receive God's promised inheritance. She will lead you to experience unparalleled personal breakthroughs that will position you to receive God's best for your life.

—**Roberts Liardon**
Best-selling author and speaker

I highly recommend her book for all who want to shift out of the ordinary and into the extraordinary life that Jesus has made available!

—**Barbara Wentroble**
Founder, International Breakthrough Ministries
Coppell, Texas

Joan Hunter is a dynamic explosion of Holy Spirit power, filled with compassion for others through the love of Jesus Christ!

—**Joshua and Janet Angela Mills**
Evangelists, New Wine International
Palm Springs, California

I love the humility, simplicity, and love I see and feel in Joan. We need more genuine ministers like her in America today.

—**Paulette Blaylock**
Senior Pastor, Landmark Christian Center
Porterville, California

Supernatural
PROVISION

Living in Financial Freedom

Supernatural
PROVISION

Living in Financial Freedom

Joan HUNTER

WHITAKER
HOUSE

SUPERNATURAL PROVISION:
Living in Financial Freedom
with CD insert

Joan Hunter Ministries
P.O. Box 777
Pinehurst, TX 77362-0777

ISBN: 978-1-60374-435-5
Printed in the United States of America
© 2010, 2011 by Joan Hunter

Whitaker House
1030 Hunt Valley Circle
New Kensington, PA 15068
www.whitakerhouse.com

Library of Congress Cataloging-in-Publication Data

Hunter, Joan, 1953–
   Supernatural provision / by Joan Hunter.
      p.   cm.
   Summary: "Equips readers to thrive in the face of uncertain economic times by trusting God as their Source and Sustainer, practicing faithful stewardship, and reaping the abundant blessings that come as a result of obedience to God"—Provided by publisher.
   ISBN 978-1-60374-435-5 (trade pbk. : alk. paper) 1. Money—Religious aspects—Christianity. 2. Trust in God—Christianity. I. Title.
   BR115.W4H86 2011
   241'.68—dc23
                              2011039248

1 2 3 4 5 6 7 8 9 10 11 ⊔⊔ 18 17 16 15 14 13 12 11

Dedication

To the faithful who are catching the vision to be a part of the end-time harvest.

To those individuals God is raising up to fund the churches and ministries that are doing the work of God.

To those who never thought they could ever get out of debt or pay off their cars and homes but did.

To all my children, whom God has blessed me with. They were there when there was nothing left after the devastation in 2000, and they rejoice with me in all that God has blessed me with during my restoration.

And especially to my daughter Charity. I had never thought about paying off my car until she encouraged me to do it. I paid it off within three months! She started me on the road to this revelation about God's miraculous provision.

Acknowledgments

I would like to acknowledge Naida Johnson Trott, RN, CWS, FCCWS, and ordained minister, who is my friend and dedicated editor. I have known Naida for almost three decades, and she has given her life in service to Jesus. She is one of the most selfless people I have ever known. She did a great job in compiling and editing this book. While she was working on it, she applied the revelation about prayer and prayed for her mate to come. After all of her praying, seeding, proclaiming, and believing, God sent her an incredible blessing—her husband, Edward Trott!

The information in this book can be used in every area of your life, including your relationships.

I would also like to thank my husband, Kelley Murrell, for his endless hours of proofing and helping me decide which stories and testimonies to include.

An extended thank-you to the Whitaker family and Whitaker House team for making this book a reality.

Contents

Foreword by Sid Roth

As a new believer, I attended a healing seminar hosted by Kenneth Hagin Sr. I knew that what he was sharing was truth, and I couldn't wait to start praying in faith for people to be healed. When I got home, I found that a close relative had developed cancer. I prayed for her healing, but she was not healed. Immediately, the devil tested me for the Word's sake, and he won. Many years later, the spiritual scales came off my eyes, and I was able again to clearly see the truth of Kenneth Hagin's teaching.

Then, the devil tried his same strategy on me with prosperity. I saw the manipulation of the prosperity teachers on television, and, frankly, I got turned off. The messenger turned me off to the message. When prosperity teachers wanted to be guests on my television show, *It's Supernatural!*, I was not interested.

Our ministry was prospering, and I also had never personally had a financial problem. I used to say that my Jewish mother took care of my every need, even as an adult, and when she was promoted to heaven, my Jewish Messiah took over. The reason I prospered was that the moment I became a believer, I learned about tithing. After that, I never considered *not* tithing.

My ministry has prospered because I have always looked for other ministries to support. I can honestly say that God has taken care of all of my financial needs and has blessed me extravagantly in the forty-plus years I have known Him. As the economy deteriorated, God continued to bless us financially. However, I have seen many believers suffer in the area of finances.

Joan Hunter has been a guest on *It's Supernatural!* many times. She has also supported our ministry financially on a monthly basis, but I was not aware of this until recently. When my producer brought me Joan's latest book on healing, I was excited to interview her again. She has had more reports of healings than any other guest I've interviewed.

Then, when my producer told me Joan had a book on financial prosperity, I was not interested—at first. Yet the Spirit of God told me to take a look. I was amazed to find out that she had come from a background of poverty. I knew her parents, Charles and Frances Hunter. Frances was an accomplished author and speaker. Even in my wildest imagination, I could not see Frances allowing her son to go to grocery stores at night to rummage through dumpsters for rotten fruit.

Next, I listened to Joan's teaching CD of the material that was developed into this book. I found out about the impossible financial problems she had faced as a single parent. I also discovered how she had believed and acted on the financial promises in the Bible with such childlike faith and seen amazing results. I felt that if she could get these results, anyone else could get the same results. Joan lists example after example of people who have achieved financial breakthroughs by applying her teaching. Her principles have even worked for people in Third World countries. Hearing about Joan's experiences has caused my own faith to soar. What she shares is absolutely contagious!

So, after listening to Joan's CD, I called my producer and said, to her surprise, "Let's do the show with Joan on finances." I know we are coming into the worst economic times in the history of the United States, but it will be the best economic times for believers in Jesus. Watch for the transfer of wealth from the sinners to the righteous. (See Proverbs 13:22.) God wants you to be a part of this great exchange. I believe Joan's book will help make the difference.

—**Sid Roth**
Host, *It's Supernatural!* television program

Introduction

I have known what it is to be in financial need. While I was growing up in south Florida, my mother, my brother, and I experienced some very tough times. Mom, a single parent, started a secretarial company to support us. Our once-a-week treat was bologna, the only meat my brother and I ate, other than whatever we were served in the school cafeteria.

I remember watching Mom hoist my brother into the dumpster behind a grocery store to retrieve a bushel of spoiled peaches. We took them home, and Mom cut off the inedible parts so that my brother and I could have a small bowl of fruit to eat.

We did not know the Lord at that time. Today, I thank Him for getting us through those years of financial hardship. In my youth, God turned total devastation and poverty into incredible blessings, and He did so again in my adult years.

If He did it for me, He will also do it for you, for He is not a respecter of persons; He shows no partiality. (See Acts 10:34 KJV, NKJV.) God does not lie. His Word is always true, His love is never ending, and His plans for us are the best. God promises to provide for all of our needs and to bless us above and beyond our wildest imaginings. (See Ephesians 3:20.)

God has an inexhaustible supply of resources to meet our every need.

You may find it difficult to believe these truths in the midst of a world in which the economy often seems to teeter on the brink of collapse. The financial forecast is seldom encouraging, and it tends to incite panic in a large portion of the world's population. Even so, God has an inexhaustible supply of resources to meet our every need. As Paul wrote to the Philippians, *"My God shall supply all your need according to His riches in glory by Christ Jesus"* (Philippians 4:19).

In the pages of *Supernatural Provision*, we will discuss this truth—and others that pertain to God's endless supply—in greater depth. For now, it's important to realize that the extent to which you will receive your inheritance of the bountiful blessings He has promised to you depends upon how you relate to Him—specifically, the degree to which you trust and obey Him with your finances. As long as you rely solely on your own efforts to earn money to pay the bills, you will not enjoy the richness of His supernatural resources. But, if you acknowledge Him as your Source and Sustainer, He will provide for you—tangibly, to meet your physical needs, and spiritually, through revelation by His Holy Spirit.

The key to receiving revelation is surrender. As you believe God and seek to know Him more—as you surrender your reliance on carnal ways and rely more and more on the power of God, rather than on what you can see or control—He opens your spiritual eyes.

As you read this book and listen to the accompanying CD, ask God for His guidance and wisdom. Ask for and receive His blessings. Open your heart to Him and His revelations. Then, *"the eyes of your understanding* [will be] *enlightened; that you may know what is the hope of His calling, what are the riches of the glory of His inheritance in the saints"* (Ephesians 1:18). True freedom comes when you recognize, know, and accept that He is guiding you and providing for your every need along the path He has planned for you.

I have experienced the loss of income, marriage, and home, yet God has been faithful without exception. I have watched God take my provisions from piddling to plentiful. He has always been there for me. I am compelled to share what I have learned with you, my brothers and sisters in Christ, so that you, too, may live in the abundance of God's provision, not by the peaks and pitfalls of the world's economy.

I have watched God take my provisions from piddling to plentiful. He has always been there for me.

Chapter 1

"Word" Economics

*Blessed is the man who trusts in the LORD, and
whose hope is the LORD. For he shall be like a tree
planted by the waters, which spreads out its roots
by the river, and will not fear when heat comes; but
its leaf will be green, and will not be anxious in the
year of drought, nor will cease from yielding fruit.*
—Jeremiah 17:7–8

When you hear the word *economics*, you probably think of
the largely secular discipline that deals with the production,
distribution, and consumption of goods and services. You may
think of the stock market, which rises and plummets in an
alarming pattern. You may think of taxes and tariffs and currency exchanges. The realm of money may seem incompatible
with faith, having little or nothing to do with the supernatural.

Yet the Christian life is not a dichotomy of material and
spiritual, natural and supernatural. Those of us who call
God our Savior and Lord know that every aspect of life has

a natural and a supernatural component—economics included. Our financial wellness matters as much to God as our physical health, and we should not look at our finances from a standpoint that's informed solely by secular investment analysts and stockbrokers. No part of your life can be understood without revelation from the Holy Spirit.

Understanding divine financial provision and the supernatural flow of money requires a personal revelation from God, just like every other area of Christian experience. Men cannot understand God's methods using the world's logic, which tells us to save x dollars each year, invest in certain funds, and otherwise make our own way. Most Christians have subscribed to worldly financial thinking: only 10 to 20 percent of all churchgoers tithe faithfully, which indicates that many do not believe that God will enable them to do more with the 90 percent they keep after tithing than with the money they save by refusing to tithe. Others are ignorant of the Bible's teachings on tithing. They have not discovered that God keeps covenant with His children and provides for their needs from His inexhaustible riches in glory, not their limited incomes.

God's economy is thriving, with enough provision for you to do everything He has planned for you.

Christians must know the difference between world economics and "Word" economics—the divine ways in which God provides for His children as they advance His kingdom on earth. His Word—the Holy Bible—is the answer book for questions about the realm of personal finances, especially as it concerns the call of God on your life. In these end times, the economy of God is not the same depressing picture that the world paints, with its buzz about deflation, inflation, recession, depression, unemployment, et cetera. His economy is thriving, with enough provision for you to do everything He has planned for you. He knows what works all the time.

A Steady Constant amid an Economy in Flux

In the world's economy, it's a "buyer's market" one day, a "seller's market" the next. The stock exchange is unpredictable, with investment brokers changing their tune every day. The threat of market crashes haunts investors everywhere, so that an atmosphere of panic and confusion permeates Wall Street and financial analysts.

Who is the author of confusion? Who is the author of scare tactics and lies? We all know that it's God's opponent, Satan. Because he is God's enemy, he is also our enemy, and he will do anything and everything to discourage Christians. If he can get us to doubt God's provision and live in paranoia about unemployment, bankruptcy, and the like, he has the upper hand.

The great thing about God's economy is, it never changes. While the world's economy is in constant flux, the principles by which God's economy operates are eternal; they do not shift according to the latest trends on Wall Street. The current economic conditions do not limit God. He doesn't have more money when stocks are soaring and less when the market tanks. *The earth is the LORD's* (Exodus 9:29); He owns it all, all the time. He could turn stones into loaves of bread if He chose to. (See Matthew 4:3–4.) He used ravens to feed the prophet Elijah. (See 1 Kings 17:6.) He supplied sustenance for Noah and the other inhabitants of the ark during the great flood. (See Genesis 6:13–9:1.) He can provide for those who trust Him in any situation.

When the enemy tries to tell you something negative, laugh out loud! If he whispers fear and paranoia into your mind, call him a liar and quote God's Word to him, just as

Jesus did when Satan was tempting Him in the wilderness. (See Matthew 4:1–11.)

Heed the True Anchor, Not the News Anchor

Most Christians read the Bible and pray when they are at a crossroads and need wisdom on what to do. Yet many of them make the mistake of seeking the Bible's wisdom for every area of life *except* their finances! They consult the Word of God for answers to questions about health, emotions, relationships, and the like, but neglect to search the ultimate source of wisdom for financial advice—with tragic results.

I know a woman whose husband could not stay away from the news. He listened to, watched, or read the news all day and long into the night. Panic invaded his mind on a daily basis and also permeated his marriage and family, and his wife was at a loss for how to deal with the spirit of fear that had taken over her home.

Sadly, many people devote much of their attention to the news, whether it's by watching TV, listening to the radio, surfing the Internet, or checking Facebook, Twitter, or other social media sites for updates. The news from these sources is almost always from man's perspective, not God's. Granted, being informed about world events is useful—how else can we know when to pray for change or when to rejoice over the fulfillment of God's promises? But the fact remains that most news broadcasts emphasize the negative and end up inciting panic and undermining our confidence.

Watch What You Lean On

How many people do you know who trust the news without question? They are totally consumed with the opinions of man as their ultimate source of knowledge; they "lean on" worldly news and then wonder why they do not have peace and joy!

Does the Bible say, "Trust in the news with all your heart, and it shall direct your path"? No! God's Word tells us, *"Trust in the LORD with all your heart, and lean not on your own understanding; in all your ways acknowledge Him, and He shall direct your paths"* (Proverbs 3:5–6). In the midst of a seesawing stock market and high unemployment, trusting in God's provision can be a challenge. The key is to be more focused on His promises—His economy, as revealed in His Word—than on the world economy.

Guard Your Ears

You may be familiar with Romans 10:17: *"Faith comes by hearing, and hearing by the word of God."* What you may not realize is that, like faith, fear also comes by hearing—listening to the news, to the world around you.

If we try to keep up with the world's financial reports and heed messages of economic doom and gloom, we are bound to become anxious and prey to fear. Fear, as you know, is the opposite of faith, and it is not from God: *"For God has not given us a spirit of fear, but of power and of love and of a sound mind"* (2 Timothy 1:7). Again, if the news is what you focus on, a spirit of fear will pervade your thoughts. Your spirit will be dominated by whatever you feed your mind.

As I wrote earlier, the "news" that bombards us 24/7 should not be our primary source of information, especially when it comes to our finances. Instead of depending on the newscasters, we should turn to the Word of God. The more we depend on the Word, the more content and confident we will be. Where do you go for answers? God's Word or the news broadcasts?

Guard Your Mind

When you spend hours surfing the Internet, reading the newspaper, and watching TV news anchors broadcast their negative messages, what will enter your mind? Negativity. Junk. Trash. Fear. Poverty.

Be careful about the thoughts you entertain. Instead of dwelling on negativity, use your God-given discernment. When the financial forecast is dire, you will be free from anxiety and fear, because the truths about God's economy—the promise of His supernatural provision and inexhaustible resources—will keep your soul at peace.

In addition, when you renew your mind (see Romans 12:2), you will have the *"mind of Christ"* (1 Corinthians 2:16). And, when you think with the mind of Christ, you end up making wise decisions based on your faith in God and your obedience to His Word.

Guard Your Tongue

Death and life are in the power of the tongue: and they that love it shall eat the fruit thereof.
(Proverbs 18:21 KJV)

It may come as a revelation to you, but your words can affect the level of your material wealth. You can bring in money by the words you use. You speak by faith and you act in obedience to the Word of God. No matter how you feel at the time or how much money you have, when you speak in faith and obey God's Word, He blesses you and your offspring.

Consider the words you speak. Are they words of peace and faith, or are they expressions of fear and panic? When you choose to fill your mind with God's truth and speak words of faith alone, you withstand the spirit of fear and dwell in the prosperity of God. If anything is blocking your income, you must pray positive words over your finances. Declare good things. Speak increase and prosperity. The words of your mouth will determine your success, not the naysaying of the newscasters.

We have this assurance in the Psalms:

Blessed is the man that walketh not in the counsel of the ungodly, nor standeth in the way of sinners, nor sitteth in the seat of the scornful. But his delight is in the law of the LORD; and in his law doth he meditate day and night. And he shall be like a tree planted by the rivers of water, that bringeth forth his fruit in his season; his leaf also shall not wither; and whatsoever he doeth shall prosper. (Psalm 1:1–3 KJV)

When we set our minds in agreement with the promises in the Word of God, we can expect incredible blessings from our Father, for He supernaturally blesses His people!

Faith for Finances in Tumultuous Times

In the midst of the housing bust and economic downturn of 2008–2009, our ministry had to relocate. On top of that, my husband, Kelley, and I moved. The logistics of such an undertaking are usually overwhelming, not to mention the added difficulty of my having to help direct the process from a distance due to my extensive travel schedule. Yes, I continued to travel wherever God sent me during this time and usually found myself out of town.

Despite the circumstances that surrounded us, our needs were met supernaturally. Our ministry has more workspace than ever before, and our new home is beautiful. We are grateful for God's blessings, and we excitedly anticipate the blessings to come as we faithfully follow His leading.

True prosperity is found in the Word of God. If we feed ourselves continually on the things of God, our souls will prosper. As our souls prosper, our bodies and minds also prosper. The effects of these blessings overflow into every corner of our lives.

Is everything in our lives perfect 24/7? No! We still live on earth and daily face challenges to overcome. However, we are so blessed that we just hop over each challenge to catch the next blessing. We listen to God's Word, speak His Word, and believe His Word.

> **When you turn to the Word of God, you receive only good news—the promises He has in store for you.**

When you turn to the Word of God, you receive only good news—the promises He has in store for you. As we have discussed, a steady diet of world news produces nothing but fear, worry, and anxiety. What will you listen to? Whose report will you believe? (See Romans 10:16–17.) Will you continue to rely on the world's economy, or will you walk into and stay within the economic principles designed by our Creator? Every day, you will make such a choice. Choose carefully.

Man may fail you, but God never will. And He is the greatest "personal financial adviser" you could hope for, because He always has your best interests in mind.

> *"For I know the plans I have for you," declares the* Lord, *"plans to prosper you and not to harm you, plans to give you hope and a future."*
> (Jeremiah 29:11 NIV)

Which will you trust? The words of man with doom and gloom, which plant seeds of doubt and disbelief, or the wonderful Word of God with its promises of abundant life?

If you answered "God's news," read on. In this book, I will reveal financial principles from the Word of God and show you the joy of putting your faith not in a paycheck or another source of income but in your ultimate Provider, the Lord God Almighty.

God has only good things for you, but you have to turn to Him and open your mind and heart to hear, discern, understand, and follow His plans for you. When you deposit faith for your finances in the bank of heaven, you will receive the greatest possible return, and His peace and prosperity will permeate your life. May it be so for you today!

Chapter 2

Created for Abundance

*If you then, being evil, know how to give good gifts
to your children, how much more will your heavenly
Father give the Holy Spirit to those who ask Him!*
—Luke 11:13

When one of my children gets a raise, do I say something like, "Oh, no! It is terrible that you got a raise"? Absolutely not! I cheer and yell! God does the same thing for us.

God Delights in the Prosperity of His Children

*Let them shout for joy and be glad, who favor my
righteous cause; and let them say continually, "Let
the LORD be magnified, who has pleasure in the prosperity of His servant."* (Psalm 35:27)

God does not take pleasure in our poverty or our hunger. He takes pleasure in our prosperity! Personally, I want Him to get a lot of pleasure through my prosperity and yours.

Have you ever heard someone say, "God is going to humble me by making me poor"? I have. Is that in agreement with His Word? No. You should not have to lose everything and live in poverty in order to develop humility.

Scripture actually teaches that the *"**love** of money"*—not money itself—*"is the root of all kinds of evil"* (1 Timothy 6:10). Having money or possessions is not evil, as long as they don't "have" you.

It is natural to desire good things for your life. You do not wake up in the morning saying, "I hope I oversleep, get a flat tire on the way to work, and spill hot coffee on my new shirt." Rather, you hope for all green lights on the way to work and no traffic on the freeway. However the lights change or however crowded the freeway may be, you can accept those things as part of life and be thankful for God's timing and protection.

> **Don't ever think that it isn't scriptural to have money. It most certainly is!**

I want you to have so much money that you couldn't give it all away, even if you wanted to, and your children and grandchildren won't be able to spend it all after you die. I want you to be able to give them anything and everything they need, including houses, and still have money left over after giving millions of dollars to the kingdom of God. It is totally scriptural to believe that your heirs will have a great inheritance. Don't ever think that it isn't scriptural to have money. It most certainly is! God wants His children to prosper.

Don't Say, "I Don't Deserve It"

God wants to bless His children, yet many of them think they don't deserve it. For some reason, they believe that poverty equals piety. No verse in the Bible says that God expects us to be poor. He wants to bless us beyond measure. John 10:10 says that He wants to bless us abundantly—not just bless us, but bless us abundantly!

Many times, God wants to bless us, yet we claim we don't need it. Or, we say no to someone who tries to bless us, never realizing that he or she is a conduit of God's goodness. The Lord frequently uses other people to deliver His blessings to us!

You need to learn how to receive, and the first step is acknowledging you are worth it. God wants to spoil you. He delights in blessing you with more than food to eat and a roof over your head.

Jesus supernaturally provided for His disciples, and He can provide a miracle for you, too. One time, He told Peter prophetically that he would find a gold coin in the mouth of a fish. (See Matthew 17:24–27.) Jesus may not supply a gold coin in the mouth of a fish for you, but He can use anything He chooses to meet your needs. He wants to supply more than you need—He desires to meet your "wants," as well. God is an awesome God, an amazingly generous Father, who wants you to live in abundance, not merely survive. He wants to be the One who meets your needs Himself.

Escape the Poverty Mind-set

Many people with a mind-set embedded in poverty or recession fully expect to experience loss, depression, and defeat. They are blind and deaf to any other information, no matter how convincing the argument. They are living with the mind-set of poverty. Many are trapped by this spirit of poverty and appear to be satisfied living below God's best.

It is possible to be free from poverty and still be trapped in the *mind-set* of poverty. People can be born-again believers but still find themselves making decisions from the viewpoint of poverty if they do not understand how Christ thinks. Some people expect to be poor and experience loss regardless of the daily blessings God is pouring over them.

The mind of Christ does not have any connection to the mind-set of poverty or the mentality that traps you in a poverty mode. Christ's kingdom is an ever-increasing kingdom, not one in a state of decline or recession.

A mind-set (spirit) of poverty will make you think that you are on your own, that you have no support when you have a need or face a "giant" in your life. Yet nothing could be further from the truth. You are never alone, for God is always with you; He will never leave you or forsake you. (See, for example, Deuteronomy 31:6, 8; Joshua 1:5.) Jesus is always accessible to help with every situation. When you have the mind of Christ, you understand that God wants to bless you abundantly in every area of your life. When you ask, God will give you more than you could ever hope for or dream.

> *Now to Him who is able to do exceedingly abundantly above all that we ask or think, according to the power that works in us.* (Ephesians 3:20)

God will do more for you than you could ever accomplish with your own wisdom or strength.

When you trust in God's provision, you will cease to depend upon your natural abilities and realize that the evening news does not have the ultimate answer. God will do more for you than you could ever accomplish with your own wisdom or strength.

Since you are reading this book, you obviously are not satisfied with just getting by and want to move up the ladder to success. Repeat this simple prayer:

Father, I thank You for giving me the power to get wealth. I break the spirit of poverty off my life and everything I do. I thank You for giving me a mind to use and the talents to accomplish what You have planned for my life.

Father, I thank You for a promotion and increase in my finances. I command any hindering forces that have been keeping me from receiving to be gone. I ask that You would bless the company that I work for. I believe they will prosper and bless me with a bonus. I want more in order to give more to Your work, Father. I thank You, Father, because You are my One and only true Source. In Jesus' name, amen.

Blessed to Be a Blessing

This most generous God who gives seed to the farmer that becomes bread for your meals is more than extravagant with you. He gives you something you can then give away, which grows into full-formed lives, robust in God, wealthy in every way, so that you can be generous in every way, producing with us great praise to God. Carrying out this social relief work involves far more than helping meet the bare needs of poor Christians. It also produces abundant and bountiful thanksgivings to God. This relief offering is a prod to live at your very best, showing your gratitude to God by being openly obedient to the plain meaning of the Message of Christ. You show your gratitude through your generous offerings to your needy brothers and sisters, and really toward everyone. Meanwhile, moved by the extravagance of God in your lives, they'll respond by praying for you in passionate intercession for whatever you need. Thank God for this gift, his gift.

(2 Corinthians 9:8–15 MSG)

God wants us to be rivers of financial prosperity that flow into the lives of others, not reservoirs that hold on to wealth indefinitely. Yes, we should each maintain a savings account, but we are not to hoard our blessings. We must allow His blessings to flow through us to others as He directs.

[Jesus] *said to* [His disciples], *"Watch out! Be on your guard against all kinds of greed; a man's life does not consist in the abundance of his possessions." And he told them this parable: "The ground of a certain rich man produced a good crop. He thought to himself, 'What shall I do? I have no place to store my crops.' Then he said, 'This is what I'll do. I will tear down my barns and build bigger ones, and there I will store all my grain and my goods. And I'll say to myself, "You have plenty of good things laid up for many years. Take life easy; eat, drink and be merry."' But God said to him, 'You fool! This very night your life will be demanded from you. Then who will get what you have prepared for yourself?' This is how it will be with anyone who stores up things for himself but is not rich toward God."*

(Luke 12:15–21 NIV)

Blessed to Support Ministries and Spread the Gospel

Again, serving God does not require a life of poverty. Think about it: spreading His Word around the world, as the Great Commission commands us to do, costs money. Christian television requires finances. Ministries across the globe have to depend on donations and offerings in order to continue the work of God's kingdom. Printing books and Bibles and producing CDs and DVDs with Christian messages and music can be costly.

God asks for different things from each person. Some are ordained to teach, some are blessed with talents to write or sing, while others are chosen to have special abilities to accumulate wealth in order to finance the kingdom (even though we can all do this to some degree). Together, all the parts of Christ's body function as a whole, utilizing His blessings in the best possible way. So, we must listen to His guidance and discern how He intends us to serve in His kingdom, which will determine how much money our particular "function" requires.

Whatever you do, work at it with all your heart, as working for the Lord, not for men, since you know that you will receive an inheritance from the Lord as a reward. It is the Lord Christ you are serving.
(Colossians 3:23–24 NIV)

Be generous: Invest in acts of charity. Charity yields high returns. Don't hoard your goods; spread them around. Be a blessing to others. This could be your last night. (Ecclesiastes 11:1–2 MSG)

If you give generously, God will bless you generously. And He blesses you generously so that you might give generously—what a beautiful cycle!

Take heed what you hear. With the same measure you use, it will be measured to you; and to you who hear, more will be given. (Mark 4:24)

God's principles work! There is no question about that fact in my heart. People who give will receive. Put others first, and God will reward you. Obedience to His voice brings untold blessings.

Again, many "Christian" teachers elevate the attributes of poverty and self-sacrifice, to the point that believers are led to think that having material possessions and financial wealth is sinful. This concept is far from scriptural truth! The key is to live with humility of spirit while working to further God's kingdom through financial gifts and service. Sacrificing one's personal desires to benefit another is commendable, of course, but God doesn't require 100 percent sacrifice from anyone, since Jesus has already given everything to purchase salvation for all mankind.

> **God blesses you so that you may bless others, and He blesses others so that they might bless you.**

You must learn that God wants to bless you. No matter how God gets it to you, all you have to do is say, "Thank You. Thank You, Jesus." He blesses you so that you may bless others, and He blesses others so that they might bless you.

You should give whenever God blesses you. Guess what? He blesses you every day, though not always monetarily. Regardless of the forms His blessings take, when you receive them, you should immediately look for a way to give back to His work.

Blessing Others Brings a Double Blessing

Just as God blesses other people through your generosity, He uses other people to bless you. So, the next time someone does something thoughtful for you or offers you a gift, recognize the person as a conduit of God's blessings. Realize, too, that as he or she gives in obedience to God, he or she is also blessed.

> *Give, and it will be given to you: good measure, pressed down, shaken together, and running over will be put into your bosom. For with the same measure that you use, it will be measured back to you.*
>
> (Luke 6:38)

The above truth is important to keep in mind, especially because the average Christian today does not know how to receive from God or from others. This tendency seems to stem from a determination to "go without" in order to avoid becoming materialistic. I can't stress this enough: Jesus never commanded us to live in deliberate poverty!

During a ministry trip to Tulsa, Oklahoma, I told one of the male team members that if he wanted to get something nice for his girlfriend, he ought to purchase it from a particular store. I had no notion of the pricing of their merchandise, but I knew the store's reputation.

When we went shopping at this store, I saw a beautiful leather business card holder with a little heart on it. I needed a new one, so I inquired about the price. It was more expensive than I felt I could afford. I did not intend to spend that much money on a business card holder. Later, on the plane going home, I felt convicted for not buying it when God said to me, "I have blessed you with finances. You liked that card holder and should have gotten it. I have blessed you so that you can have some things that you want, not just the things that you need."

Even though I needed a card case, I had decided that a less expensive one would be fine. But God had wanted to bless me by giving me enough money to afford a more expensive card holder.

So, I determined to purchase the card holder from another location of the same store, which has a presence throughout the country. Over the next month, I kept an eye out for a branch of the same store, but I never managed to find one.

I was about to leave on a trip when I stopped by my office and found a little package on my desk. I opened it and saw the credit card holder I had wanted. The card accompanying the gift read, "Love, from God." God wanted to bless me. Quite rudely, I had said no to His gift, but He used the postal service to deliver His blessing to my office, anyway. How awesome is He!

At the airport a few weeks later, I saw a branch of the store that carried the card holder. Why hadn't I seen it there before? God must have blinded my eyes. On display with the card holder was a coordinating checkbook. The woman accompanying me knew my story, and she asked me, "Would you like to have the checkbook?"

I said, "Well, I really don't need it."

She said, "Okay," but her head fell in disappointment. She wanted to bless me.

So, I said, "If you would like to buy it for me, you can."

With great enthusiasm, she replied, "Okay!"

During this experience, God spoke plainly to me about His desire to bless us, even in the "small" things. He may want to bless you with a new car. If you respond, "I don't need a new car; my ten-year-old vehicle is fine," God may say, "Okay, then I'll give it to someone else."

Years ago, a friend of mine had that same attitude. Her family had many needs. Someone came up and quietly slid some money into her hand. She responded by saying, "Oh, you need this more than I do!"

Her benevolent friend looked her straight in the eye and said, "If you don't receive my gift, you will rob me of my blessing!"

Thanks to this wise response, my friend accepted the gift gratefully, and she has continued to accept gifts graciously through the years. Even if she receives something she does not need or is not likely to use, she knows that she will encounter someone else who will need it.

Christians are to be prosperous, not poverty-stricken. When we trust in the Lord as our Source, we prosper as a testimony to His provision and shine a light of hope to a world under the shadow of doom-and-gloom financial forecasts. Let's proclaim to those around us that God is our Source and we expect His blessings every day.

> **When we trust in the Lord as our Source, we prosper as a testimony to His provision.**

Blessed to Bring Glory to God

You will be made rich in every way so that you can be generous on every occasion, and through us your generosity will result in thanksgiving to God.
> (2 Corinthians 9:11 NIV)

God will go far beyond your expectations to show you that He is alive and loves you. He wants to bless you—not because of your education or what you can do for yourself, but based on His faithfulness to fulfill His Word. When we prosper supernaturally—when we are blessed in a way that God alone could orchestrate—He is glorified. Again, it is not God's will for us to submit to evil circumstances and adopt a poverty mentality. He desires to provide for all of us in a supernatural way so that He can get all the glory. People will recognize His love and glorify Him, just as Darius and Nebuchadnezzar did when God delivered Daniel from the lions and his three friends from the fiery furnace. (See Daniel 3:28; 6:26–27.)

Blessings That Inspire Awe

> GOD *wasn't attracted to you and didn't choose you because you were big and important—the fact is, there was almost nothing to you. He did it out of sheer love, keeping the promise he made to your ancestors.* GOD *stepped in and mightily bought you back out of that world of slavery, freed you from the iron grip of Pharaoh king of Egypt. Know this:* GOD, *your God, is God indeed, a God you can depend upon. He keeps his covenant of loyal love with those who love him and observe his commandments for a thousand generations.*   (Deuteronomy 7:7–9 MSG)

I know a wonderful man of God from West Texas. One night, God gave him a dream of a detailed design. The next morning, he drew a design for a new piece of machinery. He took it to an engineering firm and said, "I want to show you something. What do you think of it?"

After looking over the design, the engineers said to him, "This is the most intricately designed piece of machinery we have ever seen. Where did you get your engineering degree? Where did you ever come up with this?"

He replied, "I got it in a dream."

One engineer asked, "You got it in a *what*?"

He repeated, "I got it in a dream."

In the end, he made millions of dollars from a God-given design. He did not receive the dream because he was an engineer. He did not have an engineering degree. He had not even passed the ninth grade. God simply gave him the dream. He obediently wrote everything down and presented it to the right company, and he was blessed with millions of dollars. In this case, God glorified Himself by granting a humble man a vision that confounded the wise. This is a great example of 1 Corinthians 1:27: *"But God has chosen the foolish things of the world to put to shame the wise, and God has chosen the weak things of the world to put to shame the things which are mighty."*

God did not stop there. Because this man was obedient, God gave him another supernatural dream. When God finds an obedient servant He can trust, He continues to bless him beyond measure!

God will do this and more for anyone who just trusts Him.

Blessed to Prove God's Faithfulness

The Word of God instructs us, *"Cast all your anxiety on him [God] because he cares for you"* (1 Peter 5:7 NIV). We are blessed when we take our eyes off the world and stop depending on man, for doing so will bring glory to God and demonstrate His faithfulness.

Let me give you an example. One day, someone told me that his family was in need of a new vehicle. I immediately said, "It's time to pray that God will give you a miracle vehicle." We prayed. Sure enough, this family purchased a new vehicle that cost $10,000 less than the retail value. It was three years old, with only 30,000 miles, and came fully loaded with leather seats and other extras. We prayed, they believed, God provided, and they received!

This is the hour for Christians to be more prosperous than ever before. We need to be bright lights to the world—shining examples of supernatural prosperity amid an atmosphere of economic doom and gloom. Let's tell others that our Source is God, so that He gets the glory when we are blessed beyond belief.

Chapter 3

Our Daily Bread

And my God shall supply all your need according to
His riches in glory by Christ Jesus.
—Philippians 4:19

A friend of mine is a private security guard. People hire him for protection when they travel, and he has been to many destinations across the globe. On one occasion, he was hired to escort two princes from a foreign country and provide their security while they were in the United States.

He met their plane at the airport and stayed with them around the clock. They checked in to a luxurious hotel that charged several thousand dollars a night per room. They always used credit cards that had no limit. Then, they would order dinner at expensive restaurants and go to various bars.

I said to my friend, "That must have been horrible for you." I thought he might have been jealous.

He replied, "No, it wasn't. It was one of the most incredible experiences I've ever had."

He told me that the princes and their entourage would fly from Texas to California just to have lunch and then fly back that night. The princes did whatever they wanted to do and never thought about how much things cost. They never worried about paying their bills or having a place to sleep at night. They always held their heads up high and their shoulders back because they knew who their father was—a king with inexhaustible funds.

Most of us cannot relate to that kind of lifestyle. However, we need to realize that we can and should live with that same level of confidence because our Father is even wealthier than the father of those princes.

The Supplier of All Our Needs

Our Father is the King of Kings and the Lord of Lords. We should not worry about where our next meal is going to come from or where we will sleep. Our "Daddy" will provide from His abundance for His obedient kids, you and me!

Therefore I say to you, do not worry about your life, what you will eat or what you will drink; nor about your body, what you will put on. Is not life more than food and the body more than clothing? Look at the birds of the air, for they neither sow nor reap nor gather into barns; yet your heavenly Father feeds them. Are you not of more value than they? Which of you by worrying can add one cubit to his stature? So why do you worry about clothing? Consider the lilies of the field, how they grow: they neither toil nor spin; and yet I say to you that even Solomon in all his glory was not arrayed like one of these. Now if God so clothes the grass of the field, which today is, and tomorrow is thrown into the oven, will He not much more clothe

*you, O you of little faith? Therefore do not worry, say-
ing, "What shall we eat?" or "What shall we drink?"
or "What shall we wear?" For after all these things the
Gentiles seek. For your heavenly Father knows that
you need all these things. But seek first the kingdom
of God and His righteousness, and all these things
shall be added to you.* (Matthew 6:25–33)

In chapter 1, I showed how we get into trouble when we
heed what the world says and not what the Word says. This is
also true in regard to our priorities—specifically, the things
we claim we need in order to survive. As we near the end
times, we need to be careful not to be counted among those
who love money and chase after anything we can afford, as
mentioned in this sobering Scripture:

*But know this, that in the last days perilous times will
come: For men will be lovers of themselves, **lovers of
money**, boasters, proud, blasphemers, disobedient
to parents, unthankful, unholy, unloving, unforgiving,
slanderers, without self-control, brutal, despisers of
good, traitors, headstrong, haughty, lovers of pleasure rather than lovers of God, having a form of god-
liness but denying its power. And from such people
turn away!* (2 Timothy 3:1–5, emphasis added)

Heaven forbid we fit this description! Let's talk about
how we can escape the dangers of materialism and keep our
focus on God with hearts of gratitude.

The Danger of Labeling "Wants" as "Needs"

Needs include things like food, housing, clothing, utili-
ties, transportation, and a source of income. Jesus told us in
Matthew 6 not to worry about these things.

What do you really need? Some people can live on very little. Jesus likely had only one pair of sandals; He didn't have twenty-plus pairs of shoes. He and His disciples traveled light. They didn't carry suitcases with four changes of clothes as they traveled from city to city. Toothbrushes, blow-dryers, and curling irons had not been invented yet. Laptops and cell phones were nonexistent. Television, radio, newspapers, and the Internet weren't available to spread the latest news, either.

Yet, consider the influence of Jesus and, later, His hand-picked team of disciples as they spread the gospel across the Middle East and Asia and into Europe. Under the oppression of the Roman Empire, Jesus and His disciples kept their focus on God, not their economic condition, and made the gospel their greatest priority. They did not allow their limitations, financial or otherwise, to stop them from spreading the Good News of salvation or the healing miracles of the Holy Spirit. God provided just what they needed to carry His message to the world.

What are the bare necessities? What are your needs? Many people believe that their "needs" include a fancy house, an expensive car, a closet full of clothes, dinner at an up-scale restaurant every evening, and an exotic vacation every year. In the pursuit of influence, connections, and the like, a person's "wants" turn into "needs" as perspective is lost and priorities are turned around.

This person "needs" success. That person "needs" a higher salary to afford luxury purchases. Someone else "needs" to be pampered and comfortable. Another "needs" prestige and attention. Many "need" a bigger home or a better car. Yet none of these things is necessary for survival.

True happiness and success can occur only when man's priorities line up with God's priorities. After all, God alone knows what is necessary for us to enjoy the "abundant life"

He intends to give us. (See John 10:10 KJV, NKJV.) What is most important to God should be most important to us, as well. Unfortunately, if someone doesn't know or believe in God, he lives in accordance with his own priorities, not God's principles—and misses out on *"life in all its fullness"* (John 10:10 TLB). An individual whose main goal is to earn money to satisfy selfish desires is far from God.

> **True happiness and success can occur only when man's priorities line up with God's priorities.**

However, when someone desires to increase his income in order to help fund the work of God, then God gets involved and provides whatever is needed for that person to succeed—whether people, supplies, or finances.

Jesus is the *"author and finisher of our faith"* (Hebrews 12:2). He knows what you need and when you need it. Just as you believe that Jesus died on the cross for you, you should also believe that He has your best interests in mind. He will provide what you need at the right time.

Be Frugal, Not Stingy toward God

Lately, we have been told by the financial gurus that we need to "cut back" in every area of life in order to survive. Some people may take this to mean that, along with denying themselves certain luxuries, such as a weekly pedicure, they also ought to decrease the amount of money they give toward God's work. Others may decide to attend church once a month instead of every week in order to save money on gas. These are not the areas in which to cut back! Remember, we are to give faithfully if we expect God to reward us.

Consider the following account of the widow, which also appears in the gospel of Luke.

Now Jesus sat opposite the treasury and saw how the people put money into the treasury. And many who were rich put in much. Then one poor widow came and threw in two mites, which make a quadrans. So He called His disciples to Himself and said to them, "Assuredly, I say to you that this poor widow has put in more than all those who have given to the treasury; for they all put in out of their abundance, but she out of her poverty put in all that she had, her whole livelihood." (Mark 12:41–44)

Jesus honored the widow for giving what she had to God. She knew the importance of giving and, even more, understood what a sacrificial gift her two coins represented. Trusting that God would supply her every need, she gave all that she had to honor Him.

> **When we make it our number one priority to fulfill God's will for our lives, everything else will fall into place, including our finances.**

We cannot afford to stop giving our tithes and offerings. God is generous toward us, and we are to be generous toward Him. Let's follow His instructions, regardless of what man says. God is our Source! He is our Father! He wants to be first in our lives and always knows what is best for us. His wisdom is always available when we ask for it. When we make it our number one priority to fulfill His will for our lives, everything else will fall into place, including our finances.

Consider your daily habits—do you purchase three to four specialty coffees a week? (Or a day?) How often do you dine at restaurants? Do you rent DVDs or watch pay-per-view movies every night? Think about cutting back in these areas instead of shirking your responsibilities to God and His kingdom.

"Oh, no!" most people would say. "I can't give up my coffee or my shows!" Some people are quite willing to cut back on spiritual things that can nourish the inner man for eternity but insist on hanging on to small pleasures and empty amusements that temporarily feed only the body or the soul. Their priorities are upside-down.

Sow Seeds of an Everlasting Harvest

Money is like seed. You use some of it to make bread to eat—that is, to support your lifestyle. And the rest you sow into good ground—the work of God's kingdom—as the Lord leads you. Doing so will produce a future harvest that enables others to hear the Good News, and it also qualifies you to receive blessings and provision from God.

The apostle Paul explained this principle to the Corinthians long ago, and it still applies to us today.

> *Now may He who supplies seed to the sower, and bread for food, supply and multiply the seed you have sown and increase the fruits of your righteousness, while you are enriched in everything for all liberality, which causes thanksgiving through us to God.* (2 Corinthians 9:10–11)

The prophet Isaiah wrote about how God would respond to those who would wait for Him and cry out to Him:

> *Then He will give the rain for your seed with which you sow the ground, and bread of the increase of the earth; it will be fat and plentiful. In that day your cattle will feed in large pastures.* (Isaiah 30:23)

What happens if you turn all your seed into "bread" and waste it on expensive habits? You rob yourself of the prosperity God intends for you. Today's society tells us that we need to have the newest gadgets, from iPads to digital cameras to smartphones, and to wear the latest fashions. "Keeping up with the Joneses" is expensive to do, since the trends are always changing.

Why not seed your money in soil that will produce a continual harvest, regardless of the latest fads and fashions? You need to plant a significant portion of your seed in the soil of God's kingdom. This principle is important to understand and put into practice. Your life literally depends on it. Do not eat all your seed. Instead, plant it so that it will multiply into a bountiful harvest of souls that have found eternal salvation.

Did you catch the other remarkable principle in the above two verses? God provides seed for the sower and rain to provide growth. If He tells you to do something, He will provide what you need to complete the task. For example, God provided sustenance for the widow of Zarephath and her son when she obeyed the prophet Elijah. (See 1 Kings 17.) And no one could forget the manna from heaven that kept the Israelites alive for forty years as they wandered around aimlessly in the wilderness.

If God tells you to do something, He will provide what you need to complete the task.

God hasn't changed. He still provides. However, you do have to cooperate with His plans and live by His principles. When your finances are lined up in agreement with the Word of God, you will be blessed—unbelievably, incredibly blessed—and you will move out of recession into possession of all God has planned for you.

Exercise Your God-Given Ability to Work

*And you shall remember the LORD your God, for it is
He who gives you power to get wealth, that He may
establish His covenant which He swore to your fathers, as it is this day.* (Deuteronomy 8:18)

Once, when I was studying this passage, God revealed
a key within that one verse of Scripture: It is *He* who gives
us the power to get wealth. He is certainly able to "give" us
wealth; however, He goes beyond just a gift and gives us the
ability and the wisdom to amass wealth for ourselves. This
ensures that we will continue to receive as a way of life. That
way, it isn't a onetime blessing; it's a source of continual provision.

Of course, God often blesses us with gifts or money that
we have not worked for, but, most of the time, *we* have to
work to generate an increase in our finances. As it says in 2
Thessalonians 3:10, *"If anyone will not work, neither shall he
eat."* God gives us the ability to obtain wealth; however, that
ability may require us to put on overalls and use some elbow
grease. In other words, we have to work!

God rewards us for industriousness—for obeying the
charge of the apostle Paul in Colossians:

*Whatever you do, work at it with all your heart, as
working for the Lord, not for men, since you know
that you will receive an inheritance from the Lord as
a reward. It is the Lord Christ you are serving.*
(Colossians 3:23–24 NIV)

Increase can come through our careers, inventions,
gifts, or inheritances. However, the foundation that under-
girds every avenue of increase is the Word of God.

Reading, speaking, believing, and obeying His principles and concepts will bring increase. Positive words, attitudes, and faith, as well as our generosity with our gifts and talents, are like seeds, which will grow and multiply into a harvest of blessings. To use another analogy, God draws us to His "spiritual university" for answers to life. We each have to choose to attend His classes and learn from each lesson He brings us. It is our choice.

Avoid the Trap of Debt

The rich rule over the poor, and the borrower is servant to the lender. (Proverbs 22:7 NIV)

God does not want us to be in debt. He knows the bondage that comes with debt. In the natural—life without God's intervention—it is nearly impossible to avoid taking on mortgages, car loans, and school loans, but if you have loans, you should try to pay them off as quickly as possible. The money you save on interest is worth every bit of hard work and sacrifice you have to make.

Being burdened down with stress trying to pay for extravagant living is not worth the consequences. If you need a new car, pray and ask God to send one to you. People give cars away all the time. I have seen it time and time again. And, as you wait for your new vehicle, try to make do with the one you have. The same applies when you desire new additions to your wardrobe: consider the clothing you already own and try to come up with some creative ensembles instead of rushing out to the mall. Likewise, check your pantry and prepare a creative meal whenever you're tempted to eat out.

These simple suggestions can help you to develop a sense of contentment and patience as you wait for God's miracles to meet your needs.

The Rewards of Hard Work and a Resilient Spirit

One of the most overlooked books of the Bible is Ruth, yet this book contains timeless truths that are pertinent to our current economic situation. When Ruth, a woman from Moab, found herself widowed, her mother-in-law, Naomi—also a widow—told Ruth and her other widowed daughter-in-law to go back to their people, since she had no means of supporting them. Yet Ruth was committed to remaining with her mother-in-law, and she returned with Naomi to her hometown of Bethlehem in Judah.

Naomi blamed God for her misfortune, and she lamented,

> Do not call me Naomi; call me Mara, for the Almighty has dealt very bitterly with me. I went out full, and the LORD has brought me home again empty. Why do you call me Naomi, since the LORD has testified against me, and the Almighty has afflicted me?
> (Ruth 1:20–21)

Whereas her mother-in-law wallowed in despair, Ruth got to work. She obtained permission from Naomi to glean grain from some neighboring fields. When the man who owned the field found out about Ruth, he showered her with favor:

> "You will listen, my daughter, will you not? [Boaz said to Ruth.] Do not go to glean in another field, nor go from here, but stay close by my young women. Let

your eyes be on the field which they reap, and go after them. Have I not commanded the young men not to touch you? And when you are thirsty, go to the vessels and drink from what the young men have drawn." So she fell on her face, bowed down to the ground, and said to him, "Why have I found favor in your eyes, that you should take notice of me, since I am a foreigner?" And Boaz answered and said to her, "It has been fully reported to me, all that you have done for your mother-in-law since the death of your husband, and how you have left your father and your mother and the land of your birth, and have come to a people whom you did not know before. The LORD repay your work, and a full reward be given you by the LORD God of Israel, under whose wings you have come for refuge." Then she said, "Let me find favor in your sight, my lord; for you have comforted me, and have spoken kindly to your maidservant, though I am not like one of your maidservants." Now Boaz said to her at mealtime, "Come here, and eat of the bread, and dip your piece of bread in the vinegar." So she sat beside the reapers, and he passed parched grain to her; and she ate and was satisfied, and kept some back. And when she rose up to glean, Boaz commanded his young men, saying, "Let her glean even among the sheaves, and do not reproach her. Also let grain from the bundles fall purposely for her; leave it that she may glean, and do not rebuke her." So she gleaned in the field until evening, and beat out what she had gleaned, and it was about an ephah of barley. (Ruth 2:8–17)

Boaz blessed Ruth with protection, with favor, with the fruit of his fields, and, ultimately, with the security of marriage when he took her as his wife. He was her "kinsman-redeemer."

In this way, he was an Old Testament type (foreshadowing) of Christ, our Redeemer.

Ruth bore Boaz a son named Obed, who would become the grandfather of King David. Isn't it amazing? God redeemed a non-Jewish woman from an idolatrous people during a time of personal crisis that was both emotional and financial, blessed her with a husband, children, and adequate wealth, and grafted her into the lineage of Jesus.

What God did then, He is still doing today. Many of us are in the same position that Ruth and Naomi were in—suffering from poverty of spirit, from lack of provision, from concern and woe. A large portion of the world is experiencing economic decline. Banks and multinational corporations are failing. Unemployment rates are high in the United States and around the globe. Currencies are being propped up artificially. You could say there is a kind of famine in the land. Yet, like Naomi and Ruth, we have a decision to make. When we face difficult circumstances, we can choose to become bitter and blame God, as Naomi did, or we can throw ourselves at the feet of Jesus, our Redeemer, and trust Him to provide for us as we walk in humble obedience to Him, similar to what Ruth did. If your attitude truly controls your "altitude," this is the time to make sure you trust in Jesus as your Savior and speak only words of faith in Him.

Father God is giving His children dreams, visions, clever inventions, and new business ideas to sustain them in the midst of these difficult economic times. Jesus, as our divine Boaz, is directing His servants, both human and divine, to make provision for those who gain favor in His eyes—His "Ruths." He gives us the power to gain wealth in totally unexpected ways.

The Lord wants to show Himself strong on the behalf of a generation that is destined to lead those who do not

> **God wants the release of His favor to be a sign and a wonder to the lost, proving that He lives and rewards those who trust Him.**

know Him out of bondage and into the freedom that comes from having a personal relationship with Him. He wants the release of His favor to be a sign and a wonder to the lost, proving that He lives and rewards those who trust Him.

It is not His desire for His children to languish in bondage to foreigners who worship other gods, as Ruth would have done in returning to Moab. He wants to deliver His people. He is calling us to occupy a position with Him that allows us to look over the heads of our enemies and see into the heavenly realms to the Source of our provision in Christ.

Every crisis, whether it's financial, emotional, spiritual, relational, or physical, has a supernatural solution that God makes available to His people, if they will only tap into His wisdom in the proper way. God wants to take us from a lifestyle of gleaning the leftovers from the efforts of the world to entering into the fullness of His holy harvest—a place of abundance, a place of usefulness and fulfillment. Let's enter in now!

Chapter 4

Giving God's Way

"Bring all the tithes into the storehouse, that there may be food in My house, and try Me now in this," says the LORD of hosts, *"if I will not open for you the windows of heaven and pour out for you such blessing that there will not be room enough to receive it. And I will rebuke the devourer for your sakes, so that he will not destroy the fruit of your ground, nor shall the vine fail to bear fruit for you in the field,"* says the LORD of hosts; *"and all nations will call you blessed, for you will be a delightful land,"* says the LORD of hosts.*
—Malachi 3:10–12

In this passage from Malachi, God challenges us to test Him. When we do, He will prove to us that He does not lie. He will do what He says He will do. He wants you to accept His offer to bless you. Isn't that awesome? He also promises to protect you from the enemy—*"the devourer."* The only prerequisite is giving faithfully to Him.

Expressing Gratitude and Obeying God

The act of giving back to God in the forms of tithes, offerings, and alms acknowledges Him as the Source of all we have and also proves that we trust Him to provide for our needs.

Of course, we can say, "Thank You, God!" to show our appreciation to the great Provider. However, merely uttering those words does not adequately express our belief in Him and His Word. The best way to thank Him is to give freely, as He guides us, through tithes, offerings, and alms to our churches, to Christian ministries, to charities, and directly to those in need. In doing this, we are not only showing Him our hearts; we are also proving to Him and to the world our faith in what He says about who He is. The act of giving back to God in the forms of tithes, offerings, and alms acknowledges Him as the Source of all we have and also proves that we trust Him to provide for our needs. Moreover, He commands us to do it!

> *You shall seek the place where the LORD your God chooses, out of all your tribes, to put His name for His dwelling place; and there you shall go. There you shall take your burnt offerings, your sacrifices, your tithes, the heave offerings of your hand, your vowed offerings, your freewill offerings, and the firstborn of your herds and flocks. And there you shall eat before the LORD your God, and you shall rejoice in all to which you have put your hand, you and your households, in which the LORD your God has blessed you.* (Deuteronomy 12:5–7)

Does God need our money? No, of course not. He owns everything. However, He does need to know that we appreciate His gifts, and He needs our obedience as a sign of our faith in His ability to provide for us. Remember, God is not after your money; He is after your heart!

God is not after your money; He is after your heart!

Furthermore, when we give money to support the servants of the Lord, we actually "help" Him to help them. Giving is fun! It's rewarding! And it's a privilege to give back to God, realizing that He trusts us to obey His voice and assist others in fulfilling His call on their lives. We don't "have to"; we "get to" bless Him with our appreciation, thankfulness, and love.

God gives us life—every breath we breathe, every heartbeat. He created the earth to sustain us—the sun to keep us warm, the rain to replenish the land. Everything He created was for our benefit. He gives us all that we have now and all that we will possess in the future. Why do people fuss over giving a small token back to Him? He is not asking for everything we have, just a small part of our "increase." When we entrust our financial futures to the Lord, we can be confident that our needs will be met.

Every deposit you make in God's heavenly bank has a guaranteed return for your future, as well as that of your descendants. This truth is included in God's Word, the Bible, which is His contract with His children. You need to read the "fine print" of your personal contract with your Creator—the details of how and why He handles your finances—and accept His revelation for your financial situation. Regardless of any uncertainties we may have about giving sacrificially, we must keep in mind that God can accomplish more with our money than we ever could on our own.

Tithes

The tithe is simply 10 percent of all you make or receive—your increase. When we tithe faithfully, or give that amount back to God, He blesses us by causing the other 90 percent to stretch even further than it would have without the subtraction of the tithe.

The practice of tithing was present before the law—including the commandment to tithe—was given to Moses. In fact, the first scriptural reference to tithing occurs in Genesis 14:18–20, which says that Abram gave Melchizedek a tithe of all he had—and it has endured ever since.

Jacob promised to give a tenth of all he had to the Lord in return for His faithful presence and provision. (See Genesis 28:20–22.)

The tithe is described as *"holy"* in Leviticus:

And all the tithe of the land, whether of the seed of the land or of the fruit of the tree, is the LORD's. It is holy to the LORD....And concerning the tithe of the herd or the flock, of whatever passes under the rod, the tenth one shall be holy to the LORD.
(Leviticus 27:30, 32)

If something is holy, it belongs to the Lord. So, the tithe is the part of your possessions that goes back to Him. You are a steward of everything God has given to you, and a faithful steward tithes 10 percent and then distributes the remainder among his bank account, to be saved for future expenses; his wallet, to meet the expenses of every day living; and the church or other Christian organizations, to support them financially.

I believe there are two reasons for the tithe: one that is natural, and one that is supernatural. In Malachi 3:10, God commands His people to bring their tithes into the *"store-house."* The equivalent of the storehouse for us today would be the church where we are fed spiritually on a regular basis. Why should we do this? So that there will be *"food"* in the house of God. (See verse 10.) When everyone contributes his or her portion, there are plenty of resources available to accomplish His work. So, we see that the natural reason for tithing is to meet the physical needs of the church, by paying the utility bills, providing for the staff's salaries, funding outreach events, replenishing supplies, and so forth. The tithe helps to cover the day-to-day expenses the church incurs. These things are necessary in today's society. We like to go to a church where the lights are on, the sound system works, and there is running water in the bathrooms and water fountains.

The supernatural reason for tithing is that it benefits you. There are blessings that come from your obedience. In Malachi 3:10–12, you will see that the promise of God's protection is directly connected to your tithe. When you tithe in obedience, He rebukes the devourer, Satan, and his minions, who are determined to derail you from your pursuit of God's purpose for your life.

God has made us a promise. When we tithe 10 percent, He will multiply the remaining 90 percent to meet our needs. Our obedience proves that we worship Him and not our money.

Offerings

Going a step further, the Holy Spirit will prompt us to give an offering—an amount above, or in addition to, our tithe. This is yet another opportunity to give to Him in obedience and entrust all that we have to Him, because all of it came from Him in the first place.

During most church services, part of the worship is called the "offering." Sometimes, it is called a "freewill offering."

Again, an offering is an amount above and beyond your 10 percent tithe that you give to God. When the Holy Spirit prompts you to give toward a specific need in the church or to a particular ministry, your gift is considered an offering. The donations given to Christian evangelists, speakers, teachers, artists, and TV ministries also qualify as offerings.

A specific offering known as the "firstfruits" offering comes from a biblical command (see, for example, Exodus 23:19; Leviticus 2:12; Deuteronomy 18:4) and is given at the beginning or the end of the year, over and above the usual tithes and offerings. What you give "first" to God will bring a special blessing from Him on everything else you do from then on.

> *If the part of the dough offered as firstfruits is holy, then the whole batch is holy; if the root is holy, so are the branches.* (Romans 11:16 NIV)

> *Honor the LORD with your possessions, and with the firstfruits of all your increase; so your barns will be filled with plenty, and your vats will overflow with new wine.* (Proverbs 3:9–10)

One easy and practical way to fulfill the spirit of the firstfruits offering is to write a check for your tithe "first," not after all the other bills are paid. Your commitment to God takes top priority and is given first. When you honor Him above everything else, your money will seem to stretch to cover all the other expenses.

Alms

Alms can include monetary gifts; however, alms can be more than just money. Over and above tithes and offerings, alms are given to the poor and needy and include such items as food, clothing, and supplies.

> *If there is among you a poor man of your brethren, within any of the gates in your land which the LORD your God is giving you, you shall not harden your heart nor shut your hand from your poor brother, but you shall open your hand wide to him and willingly lend him sufficient for his need, whatever he needs....For the poor will never cease from the land; therefore I command you, saying, "You shall open your hand wide to your brother, to your poor and your needy, in your land."*
>
> (Deuteronomy 15:7–8, 11)

> *He who has pity on the poor lends to the LORD, and He will pay back what he has given.*
>
> (Proverbs 19:17)

In biblical times, long before banks were established, it was common for people to barter goods and services rather than pay for them with actual currency. In similar manner, tithes and offerings in the forms of animals from the flocks and produce from the fields were brought to the priests by those who were obedient to God.

Today, most churches, Christian ministries, and charities gain little benefit from live animals or trucks filled with corn and wheat. In the modern world, cash functions better because it can more easily be applied to the area of need and keep the gospel spreading around the world. Even so, supplies and other items remain popular forms of alms.

For example, when I traveled with a team to Haiti to feed the spiritually and physically starved people, our efforts would have been classified as almsgiving. We all gave freely of our time, money, energy, comfort, convenience, and love to those who literally had lost everything they had. To them, even a warm hug was a treasure. Living with so much, we often take such simple gestures for granted.

Alms include those simple little things that you can do or give spontaneously without any anticipation of return or recognition. At Christmas, you may choose to donate toys for children you will never see or meet. You might purchase a gift card for a family in need. In obedience to God's voice, you may feel led to write a check or give a gift to a stranger at church or at the grocery store.

The Bible gives us a good example of someone who was blessed because of his generosity in almsgiving. Acts 10 talks about a centurion—a *"devout man"* named Cornelius—*"who feared God with all his household, who gave alms generously to the people, and prayed to God always"* (verse 2). An angel appeared to him, told him, *"Your prayers and your alms have come up for a memorial before God"* (verse 4), and directed him to summon the apostle Peter to speak with him and his family, who were Gentiles. (See verses 5–6.) As a result of Peter's explaining the Good News to them, Cornelius and his household came to salvation and were filled with the Holy Spirit. (See Acts 10:24–48.) Cornelius had given freely of his wealth on behalf of others and, as a result, received a priceless gift: salvation and the Holy Spirit's indwelling.

Seeding in Obedience

It has been said time and time again, "If it is not enough to meet your need, it is enough to be your seed." In obedience, you plant your seed by sowing it when and where God tells you to.

Seeds planted in a garden grow into plants. Financial seeds, sown or planted into the supernatural, reap finances in the natural. This is not a get-rich-quick scheme; it is how God blesses obedience. Regardless of the dollar amount, when you give out of obedience to God, He will bless you in return, as we discussed briefly in chapter 1.

> *"Bring all the tithes into the storehouse, that there may be food in My house, and try Me now in this,"* says the Lord *of hosts, "if I will not open for you the windows of heaven and pour out for you such blessing that there will not be room enough to receive it."*
>
> (Malachi 3:10)

"Baby" (new) Christians are to "test" God, just as He instructs us in His Word. Are you ready to "prove" God? He has already given you seeds to sow through tithes, offerings, and alms. Again, your seed does not always need to be in the form of cash. If you think you don't have any monetary seed to sow, place something you *do* have in the offering plate, such as a compact or a pen. Consider volunteering your time and talents to meet a need within your church. God knows the talents He has blessed you with, and He will open doors of opportunity for you to use them to serve others. Watch for and expect opportunities to give to Him in unique ways. God wants to bless you. He is going to free you up to do what He has called you to do.

Watch for and expect opportunities to give to God in unique ways.

When you're sowing financially with cash or a personal check, how do you determine how much you should sow? Often, I practice what I like to call "scriptural giving."

Scriptural Giving

I make a habit of giving offerings in faith for a specific need. What I call "scriptural giving" is one of the most powerful giving tools that I can share with you. Let me explain what I mean by scriptural giving. It's basically a financial application of the practice of agreeing with God's Word, as we are taught to do in Matthew 18:19–20: *"Again I say to you that if two of you agree on earth concerning anything that they ask, it will be done for them by My Father in heaven. For where two or three are gathered together in My name, I am there in the midst of them."* Scriptural giving is a means of using our money in agreement with God's Word.

You begin by identifying your need—for example, perhaps you are ill, and you desire to trust God for healing. Once you have identified your need, you then search the Scriptures for verses that pertain to it. So, if I needed healing, I might select Jeremiah 30:17: *"'For I will restore health to you and heal you of your wounds,' says the Lord."* Finally, you stand on that verse in faith while you are waiting for God's answer, and, to reinforce your faith, you seed a corresponding amount. Using the example of Jeremiah 30:17, I might write a check for $30.17 to place in the offering plate.

There are certain verses, such as John 3:16, that stick in our memories. Many people have a "life verse" or a favorite passage that they hold on to during times of crisis. Again, in the final step of scriptural giving, you not only stand on a verse; you seed, or give to God, using the reference as your guide.

When you write a check for a corresponding amount, it will remind you of the particular Scripture on which you are standing in faith. Later on, when you receive the cancelled check or see the amount listed on a bank account statement, you will again be reminded of that Scripture and of what you are trusting God to do. And, when you plant your seed offering with God's Word for a specific purpose, it will come back to you having accomplished everything it was sent to do. (See Isaiah 55:11.) It will be multiplied back to you repeatedly.

Match Your Seed to Your Need

A woman came to a healing seminar where I was preaching on Deuteronomy 1:11: *"May the LORD God of your fathers make you a thousand times more numerous than you are, and bless you as He has promised you!"* On Friday night, she gave a seed of $111, believing in faith that she would be able to afford to go on more missions trips in the future. The next day, she received a telephone call saying that her mortgage had been cancelled. Talk about a blessing!

Do you know someone in the military or a missionary serving in a dangerous part of the world? Psalm 91 is a powerful Scripture about protection. A friend of mine seeded $91 for the safety of his son-in-law, who was serving in the military, and what happened next is very interesting.

This young man was serving overseas, and his position required that he work with jet fuel on a daily basis. One day, a fuel container burst, dousing him with a dangerous amount of fuel. He was immediately put under a shower and scrubbed with iron bristles from the top of his head to the soles of his feet. Then, the doctors put him in a drug-induced coma and hooked him to an intravenous feed to flush the toxins out of his body. On top of all that, the fuel had blinded him.

All of these precautionary treatments caused the young soldier to miss the daily phone call he had scheduled with his wife, the daughter of my friend. The appointed time came and passed; he didn't call, he didn't call, he didn't call. Needless to say, his wife became very worried.

Her concern soon escalated into full-blown panic. She happened to be at my house the day this occurred, and so I also experienced her emotional upheaval.

When the young man was finally able to call his wife to explain what had happened, I quickly prayed, "Father, this young man's father-in-law seeded $91 for his protection, and this situation does not line up with Your Word. I speak his eyesight be restored, and I command anything bad that has happened because of this accident to go."

The next words his wife heard were exciting. His eyes had opened up immediately, and his sight had been restored! Glory to God!

God hears our prayers and answers them, oceans away, sometimes within seconds. Don't ever limit Him by doubting what He can do!

> **Don't ever limit God by doubting what He can do!**

If you have a son or daughter who is not serving God, consider seeding $49.25 as you stand on the promise of Isaiah 49:25: *"and I will save your children."*

You cannot purchase salvation, healing, or anything else from God—I know that. However, you can seed an amount that is significant in its correspondence to a Scripture that pertains to what you are praying for and believing God will give you. Seeding scripturally adds significance to the dollar amount of your gift.

I have instructed people to plant a seed specifically for the salvation, recommitment, and/or restoration of a prodigal child. Soon afterward, their son or daughter has walked down the aisle of the church, ready to dedicate his or her life to Jesus. This has happened hundreds of times.

I know people who have adopted this practice as their number one strategy for giving. Many people have acted upon this instruction by seeding $111, in accordance with Deuteronomy 1:11, a verse I shared before. Some seed $111.11 a month. These people are receiving so much in return that they hardly get their seed back into the ground before God blesses them again. Seed $111.11, $1,111.11, or any variation of 11—whatever you can do, even if it is $11.11 or $1.11. Ask God to direct you where to put the decimal point.

Divine Mathematics

One plus one (1 + 1) equals two (2); however, one *and* one is eleven (11). (See Deuteronomy 1:11.) God's math doesn't always match up with mathematicians' logic, because *"the foolishness of God is wiser than men..."* (1 Corinthians 1:25). The revelation of scriptural giving has been powerful. I have seen it work in my own life, as well as in the lives of others.

So, find a Scripture verse that fits your need. You may even find more than one verse. Stand on God's Word. Give to Him in faith, and the circumstance for which you are seeding in faith will line up with that verse of Scripture. His Word is His promise.

Remember, you are seeding and coming into alignment with a specific Scripture verse. If you are believing God for protection, seed $91! If you do not have $91 available at this time, then give $9.10 or 91 cents.

If people are coming against you, seed $54.17 as you repeat these words: *"No weapon formed against* [me] *shall prosper"* (Isaiah 54:17).

Another popular verse for scriptural giving is Isaiah 49:25, which I mentioned earlier: *"But thus says the LORD: '...I will contend with him who contends with you, and I will save your children.'"*

I instructed a couple to give a seed of $49.25 for a son who was separated from his wife. Their son and daughter-in-law are now reunited and doing great. God is so amazing!

Isaiah 49:25 is also a great verse to stand on if somebody comes after you, either verbally or with a legal situation. Seed $49.25, stand in faith, and watch God turn the situation around.

This principle has always worked for me. The success I have experienced in my own life and witnessed in others' lives increases my faith in scriptural giving. If you want to give $100, invoke Psalm 100 as a sort of fertilizer to stimulate the fruition of a financial blessing. Whatever you choose to do, and whatever amount you decide to give, seed your offering with a supporting Scripture and watch how God responds.

Here are some additional ideas to consider. If you desire greater wisdom and revelation, seed $117.19, based on the following passage:

> ...[may] *the God of our Lord Jesus Christ, the Father of glory, give to you the spirit of wisdom and revelation in the knowledge of Him, the eyes of your understanding being enlightened; that you may know what is the hope of His calling, what are the riches of the glory of His inheritance in the saints, and what is the exceeding greatness of His power toward us who believe, according to the working of His mighty power.* (Ephesians 1:17–19)

If you are believing for a spouse, seed $31, in line with Proverbs 31, which is the picture of an ideal, biblically based marriage. A friend of mine did this, and she is now counting down the days until her wedding. She is engaged to a wonderful man of God, and they plan to do more and more for His kingdom as they unite their homes and lives.

I also like to seed $55.11, in accordance with Isaiah 55:11: *"My word...that goes forth from My mouth...shall not return to Me void, but it shall accomplish what I please, and it shall prosper in the thing for which I sent it."* The Bible says that God's Word shall not return empty or without effect. Stand on this verse as you prepare to receive whatever God has spoken to you. Name your seed, plant it in good soil, and wait in faith. What are you believing God for? Be specific! Be detailed in your request! His promises are not wasted words. Your seed will return a harvest. It will come back to you supernaturally.

Whatever your situation, if you are planning to give an offering, prayerfully ask, "God, how much do You want me to give?" If the amount He moves you to seed does not have a matching Scripture reference, do not worry about it. Simply give as He directs. However, if you are believing God for a specific situation, search the Scriptures for a verse you can align your offering with and stand on in faith. Then, your seed, planted in faith, will open the windows of heaven (see Malachi 3:10), and God's blessings will pour out in abundance over and above anything you can hope or think. (See Ephesians 3:20.)

Chapter 5

The Power of Partnership

*He who sows sparingly will also reap sparingly,
and he who sows bountifully will also reap bountifully. So let each one give as he purposes in his
heart, not grudgingly or of necessity; for God loves
a cheerful giver.*
—2 Corinthians 9:6–7

Many people believe that once their money goes into the offering plate, the story is over. Yet the impact of your financial gifts, whether tithes, offerings, or alms—as well as the blessings you receive as a result—endures long after the offering plate has been passed. God blesses your immediate contribution, of course, but the future blessings will be untraceable.

Think of a stone you toss into a pond. There is an immediate reaction—a series of rings spread out from the point of entry into the water. But it doesn't stop. The ripples go on and on, spreading out far away from the center of the circle.

Now, picture yourself putting an offering into the plate. That simple act sets off a sequence of events, like concentric rings in a pond, that is far-reaching. Added together, our gifts fund the spread of the gospel across the continent and around the world. Every dime, every dollar, is a vital brushstroke in the picture God is painting—a picture of a world in which *"every knee should bow, of those in heaven, and of those on earth, and of those under the earth, and...every tongue should confess that Jesus Christ is Lord, to the glory of God the Father"* (Philippians 2:10–11). This masterpiece comes closer and closer to completion as God's children partner with each other, as well as with local and worldwide ministries, to spread His healing Word to the hurting, the sick, and the unsaved.

Partners Help to Steer the "Ship"

Once, in a church where I was ministering, the pastor shared something profound that changed the way I look at partnerships. He explained that one way the dictionary defines *partner* is "the wooden framework used to strengthen a ship's deck at the point where a mast or other structure passes through it." *Merriam-Webster's 11th Collegiate Dictionary* words it as follows: "one of the heavy timbers that strengthen a ship's deck to support a mast."

There is a remarkable parallel between a ship's partner and those individuals who partner with a ministry by supporting it financially. For example, the purpose of the partners on a ship is to reinforce the masts. In the case of a sailing ship, the masts hold up the sails and rigging, which catch the wind that propels the ship on its course. In similar manner, the partners of a ministry support and strengthen it so that it may catch the "wind"—the Holy Spirit—and move throughout the earth, spreading the Good News.

Just as partners are vital to the successful voyage of a ship at sea, ministry partners are vital to the success of every ministry that seeks to fulfill the Great Commission. (See, for example, Matthew 28:16–20.) Christian ministries are touching a multitude of nations as they venture forth in faith to the four corners of the globe. God has affirmed the preaching of His Word with signs and wonders. (See Acts 14:3.) Salvation and healing have been brought to many, and believers are being equipped to do the work of the kingdom.

> *And He Himself gave some to be apostles, some prophets, some evangelists, and some pastors and teachers, for the equipping of the saints for the work of ministry, for the edifying of the body of Christ.*
>
> (Ephesians 4:11–12)

Without the support of our partners, those of us with ministries would not be able to take the gospel to the ends of the earth. While not all of our partners are able to travel the world with us, they uphold us faithfully through their prayers and financial gifts.

Partners Inherit an Equal Share of Blessings

The word *partner* also means "one that shares: partaker." This definition invokes the idea of a joint heir, which is also the way you and I relate to Jesus Christ. (See Romans 8:16–17.) In terms of partnering with ministries, being a joint heir means sharing in the inheritance, or the fruits, due to the missionary or minister (the heir). Every time the ministry you support brings another soul to salvation, sees another sick person healed, or trains another minister to carry the gospel message around the world, an eternal deposit is made in your heavenly account, as well as in the accounts

> **The blessings that belong to a ministry belong to its partners, as well, because of their status as joint heirs.**

of the other partners of that ministry. The blessings that belong to a ministry belong to its partners, as well, because of their status as joint heirs. They, too, share in the outpouring of God's blessings.

Father God intends us to support each other as He steers our "ship" (the church) through stormy seas to a peaceful harbor. He is our heavenly captain, and as we freely give of our resources and ourselves to His purposes, we receive all we need. Everyone on the ship partakes of the same eternal rewards as those who are the ship's "officers." As a partner with a healing ministry, for example, you become a part of every healing service. Everyone who is healed, saved, trained, or equipped to minister healing to others is credited to your account because of your support.

Functions of a Partner

Every believer has an important part to play in the body of Christ and the work of the kingdom. Each of us is a key piece of the big picture—the puzzle that is being assembled to show God's perfect plan for His world.

> *For in fact the body is not one member but many. If the foot should say, "Because I am not a hand, I am not of the body," is it therefore not of the body? And if the ear should say, "Because I am not an eye, I am not of the body," is it therefore not of the body? If the whole body were an eye, where would be the hearing? If the whole were hearing, where would be the smelling? But now God has set the members, each one of them, in the body just as He pleased.*

And if they were all one member, where would the body be? But now indeed there are many members, yet one body. And the eye cannot say to the hand, "I have no need of you"; or again the head to the feet, "I have no need of you." (1 Corinthians 12:14–21)

While some partners may be able to embark on missions trips organized by the ministry they support, others offer their help behind the scenes, yet their roles are no less important.

Faithful Prayers

The faithful prayers of partners allow the wind of the Holy Spirit to "puff the sails" and propel a ministry forward so that thousands are saved, healed, delivered, and empowered. And the blessings enjoyed by each fruitful ministry return to its partners, as well!

An element of the power of partnership lies in the principle of agreement. When people work in agreement with each other, their strength is multiplied, not just added together. Amos 3:3 says, *"Can two walk together, unless they are agreed?"*

Disagreement separates, especially disagreement with God's Word, which is an act of disobedience that results in destruction and loss. Agreement, on the other hand, solidifies and unites. Enthusiasm and encouragement among people with common goals can produce miracles. Positive reinforcement and validation strengthen and support the entire organization. Agreeing with God and His Word whisks you into His blessings of joy, peace, and love.

> **Enthusiasm and encouragement among people with common goals can produce miracles.**

Partners who intercede on a ministry's behalf believe what Jesus said in Matthew 18:19–20: *"If two of you agree on earth concerning anything that they ask, it will be done for them by My Father in heaven. For where two or three are gathered together in My name, I am there in the midst of them."*

Generous Gifts

What you give to a ministry for its work of advancing the kingdom, God will return to you, many times over.

Give, and it will be given to you: good measure, pressed down, shaken together, and running over will be put into your bosom. For with the same measure that you use, it will be measured back to you.
(Luke 6:38)

Several years ago, a family volunteered to work with my parents, Charles and Frances Hunter, who had a well-known healing ministry. Two daughters in that family offered to watch some small children while those children's parents attended one of the healing services. When these parents came to pick up their children, they blessed the two girls with $2 apiece.

Surprised, the girls immediately took the gifts to their parents. When asked what they wanted to do with these unexpected gifts, the girls agreed to give all of the money to God. They seeded that small amount into Hunter Ministries.

The following day, an older woman came up to the girls at the motel pool and said, "I don't get to see my grandchildren very often. You two look like such nice girls that I want to give you something." She pulled out two $20 bills and gave one to each of the speechless girls.

The girls went running down the hall to share their "miracle" with the family. "It works! It works!" they exclaimed. "God multiplied our two dollars!" They have never forgotten their first experience of giving all they had to a loving Father and receiving His multiplied blessings. And, throughout the years, they have planted their seed into good soil, again and again.

You Reap What You Sow

God has a special provision for those who participate in a ministry through partnership. Your partnership with a ministry will produce miracles—again, not only in the lives of the multitudes who are blessed by the ministry, but in your life, as well!

> *"Whoever calls on the name of the LORD shall be saved." How then shall they call on Him in whom they have not believed? And how shall they believe in Him of whom they have not heard? And how shall they hear without a preacher? And how shall they preach unless they are sent? As it is written: "How beautiful are the feet of those who preach the gospel of peace, who bring glad tidings of good things!"*
> (Romans 10:13–15)

As a partner, you put yourself in a position to receive the overflow from God's miracle-working power; you receive the anointing of the Holy Spirit as it is released through others. In short, you reap what you sow.

> *But this I say: He who sows sparingly will also reap sparingly, and he who sows bountifully will also reap bountifully.* (2 Corinthians 9:6)

Sow into the release of financial, spiritual, and healing miracles for others, and you will reap in kind. Seed planted in the fertile soil of fruitful ministries grows to produce a bumper crop at harvest time. Those who give obediently receive unspeakable blessings in return.

Becoming a Partner

You might choose to partner with a particular ministry if it has had an impact on your life or simply because you desire to help touch the lives of others while building an army of equipped believers worldwide. When you partner with a fruitful ministry, you can reach countless people with the good news of the gospel and the healing power of God, with signs, wonders, and miracles.

> *Not that I seek the gift, but I seek the fruit that abounds to your account. Indeed I have all and abound. I am full, having received from Epaphroditus the things sent from you, a sweet-smelling aroma, an acceptable sacrifice, well pleasing to God. And my God shall supply all your need according to His riches in glory by Christ Jesus.* (Philippians 4:17–19)

A true partnership or agreement is similar to a covenant, such as the covenant formed between David and Jonathan. (See 1 Samuel 18:1–4.) What happens to one affects the other. When you choose to join with one of God's children, be it a minister, an evangelist, a pastor, a spouse, or a fellow believer, you must be aware that his or her actions and behavior will affect you. Exercise wisdom and discernment before joining with someone, so that you may both enjoy God's blessings.

Principles of Prudent Partnering

When visiting another church or attending a special service, many people toss a token amount of money into the offering plate out of habit or a sense of duty. Don't be one of them! This is a time for exercising wisdom and discernment in regard to where you are planting your valuable seed.

Plant Your Seed in Good Soil

Whenever and wherever you give, you need to make certain you plant your seed in good soil. Do some research. You would not send your children to a school with a reputation of producing poorly educated graduates. You want your children to spend their school years in an institution where they will learn what they need to know to be successful in life.

Similarly, you would not deliberately purchase nutritionally deficient food to feed to your family. Your loved ones would not grow or thrive. Instead, they would probably become ill and possibly even die from poor nutrition. Buying or investing in less than the best would be a waste of your hard-earned money.

Rely on God's wisdom and direct your offerings to a ministry where they will have the maximum effect on the growth of His kingdom.

Your giving to God should follow the same principle. Sow your seed where you know it will grow! There are many fruitful ministries and missionaries in need of financial support. Researching their statements of faith or the work they are doing is not difficult, as most of them maintain Web sites or blogs on the Internet and/or publish complimentary newsletters or magazines. You might also consider asking to see their Form 990, if they're able to provide one, or simply request a copy of their financial report. Find out about their missions giving. Ask about their goals and what they have planned. Rely on God's wisdom and direct your offerings to a ministry where they will have the maximum effect on the growth of His kingdom.

If you've been depositing seed in a church or ministry where nothing is happening, you have been planting your finances into what I call "dead ground." There will be a "crop failure" because your seed will not grow or prosper in that soil.

You would not throw seeds in rocky soil, where nothing can grow or thrive. A harvest would be impossible. The same principle applies to your tithes and offerings. Ask God where He would have you plant your seed. He knows where the best fertilized soil is located. He knows where the seed will multiply into an abundant harvest.

Prayerfully Select Your Home Church

Do you know that you know that you know that the church you attend is where God wants you? Does the preaching of the Word minister to your heart? Does the pastor speak as if he or she has "read your mail"? In other words, do the messages relate to the issues you have been asking God about lately? Are you drawn to the church on a regular basis to be spiritually nourished, to receive prayer, and to find peace? Is there a place for you to serve and share God's love and Word? Are you excited to go to this particular house of the Lord?

Don't choose a church because it is close by or because your family has attended there for multiple generations. God sometimes moves His "kids" to new places. Life isn't meant to be stagnant. Just as your spiritual life changes as you grow from a baby Christian into a mature servant of the Lord, your church home may change, as well. One pastor may start you on your Christian journey, another encourage you through your "teenage" years of growth, and yet another challenge you to "graduate" into the deeper things God wants you to learn and experience.

So, ask yourself these questions regarding the church you attend or are considering attending: Are people getting saved? Are they being set free and delivered? Are the sick getting healed? Is there obvious growth within the church and among people who attend regularly? Does the church minister to all age groups? Is there joy, love, and peace? Are the fruits of the Spirit in operation? Are missionaries supported generously by the church?

At our church, for example, we see people healed every week. We minister to thousands every day in our meetings and through books, teaching materials, and e-mails. God is doing incredible things! Testimonies are received daily at the ministry office.

A few years ago, a lady named Lucy came up to me in Portersville, California. She had been diagnosed with stage IV lung cancer and was not expected to live. I laid hands on her, cursed the cancer, and spoke a new set of lungs into her body.

She went back to her doctor two weeks later. The doctor took X-rays, examined them very closely, and came to her with a look of bewilderment on his face. He said, "I don't know what you did, but you have two new lungs!" It was exciting to see her the following year, totally healed. Praise God!

When you give your seed to a church or a ministry where miracles are happening, you can expect to see miracles in your finances and personal ministry, as well. You will share in the anointing of that ministry. In contrast, give to a church that isn't doing anything of real spiritual value, and your seed will be starved and die. That church will receive your seed and use it; however, the seed won't reproduce supernaturally.

You will have wasted your hard-earned money. And you may feel like the church has "taken" your finances.

Find a church that is alive and working actively to spread God's Word and reach out to others with the message of salvation.

Evaluate Charitable Organizations

Many people give financial donations to various charities and nonprofit organizations. If you are thinking about doing that or are already in the habit of doing so, I simply caution you to pray about it. Make sure God tells you where to plant your seed. Do your research. Listen and give where, when, and how much God tells you to give.

Occasionally, the Lord may lead you to give what you feel is an exorbitant amount of money to a church, ministry, or charitable organization that meets the aforementioned conditions and about which you have peace. In those cases, know that He alone would make such a request. Satan will never ask you to support a Christian ministry or to position yourself to receive a wonderful blessing from God. When God asks you to do something extraordinary, He intends to give you an incredible miracle in response to your obedience.

> **When God asks you to do something extraordinary, He intends to give you an incredible miracle in response to your obedience.**

When God tells you to give offerings or alms to the poor, you can be sure He is tearing down the hindrances to your financial prosperity. He always supplies the provision necessary to complete what He has planned. If He is telling you to plant something special, it's because He has something special planned for you. Your seed will prepare the fields for a unique harvest.

Never Underestimate the Impact of Your Giving

God is pouring out His blessings on us. As this book is being written, the property on which our ministry is located is covered with beautiful grass that is being used to nourish some very hungry cows. Soon, that land will have buildings that will hold spiritually hungry people called by God to be fed, nourished, trained, and sent out to the four corners of the world to minister to the sick, hungry, and lost.

We have a big vision. We do not want a little building in a strip mall where we feed a few people. We want facilities that allow us to minister to, spiritually feed, and train hundreds of people on a regular basis. Life seems to move at a faster and faster pace as we approach the end times. In these days, we need as many people as possible actively ministering to the lost. We need to optimize our efforts and our offerings. Our ministry believes in multiplication, not just addition.

Yet, often, we all have to do things one step at a time, one person at a time. It always starts with a simple seed, planted in faith. There is a reaction to every action, no matter how small. Remember the image of a stone thrown into a pond. Such a simple action produces long-lasting effects. Imagine what an offering can do and how far it will go in God's world. The anointing on your gift can take you around the world and back, touching millions of other people. What can stop the anointing from coming back to you?

Agree and partner with those who stand on God's promises of prosperity so that you may enjoy His bounty and success. Welcome His Word and His promises!

In case you haven't read the end of the Book yet, God wins! And, as joint heirs with Jesus—as partners with Him in God's plan to redeem the world—we share in His victory.

Chapter 6

The Harvest of Obedience

When you have eaten and are full, then you shall bless the LORD your God for the good land which He has given you. Beware that you do not forget the LORD your God by not keeping His commandments, His judgments, and His statutes which I command you today, lest; when you have eaten and are full, and have built beautiful houses and dwell in them; and when your herds and your flocks multiply, and your silver and your gold are multiplied, and all that you have is multiplied; when your heart is lifted up, and you forget the LORD your God...; then you say in your heart, "My power and the might of my hand have gained me this wealth." And you shall remember the LORD your God, for it is He who gives you power to get wealth, that He may establish His covenant which He swore to your fathers, as it is this day....The LORD will greatly bless you in the land which the LORD your God is giving you to possess as an inheritance; only if you carefully obey the voice

of the LORD your God, to observe with care all these commandments which I command you today.
(Deuteronomy 8:10–14, 17–18; 15:4–5)

No matter how you feel, no matter how much money you have in your bank account, God blesses you when you are obedient to Him, especially insofar as your finances are concerned. In the book of Deuteronomy, God gave His people a litany of instructions. We explored the instructions that pertain to finances in chapter 4 of this book. While God rewards our generosity with financial blessings, His goodness extends and spills over into every area of our lives—our health, relationships, careers, and so forth.

The Blessings of Obedience

Later on in Deuteronomy, in chapter 28, the Lord delineates the blessings you will receive if you *"...diligently obey the voice of the LORD your God"* (verse 1). Verse 2 goes on to say, *"These blessings shall come upon you and overtake you."*

In other words, you do not have to "get lucky" to experience good things in your life. Blessings are a guarantee for those who *"keep the commandments of the LORD your God and walk in His ways"* (verse 9).

Let's look at an instance where obedience to God resulted in an abundant harvest. Jesus was ministering by the sea, when...

[Jesus] *said to Simon, "Launch out into the deep and let down your nets for a catch." But Simon answered and said to Him, "Master, we have toiled all night and caught nothing; nevertheless at Your word I will let down the net." And when they had done this, they caught a great number of fish, and their net was breaking. So they signaled to their partners in the other boat to come and help them. And they came and filled both the boats, so that they began to sink. When Simon Peter saw it, he fell down at Jesus' knees, saying, "Depart from me, for I am a sinful man, O Lord!" For he and all who were with him were astonished at the catch of fish which they had taken.* (Luke 5:4–9)

Because Simon Peter obeyed the words of Jesus, he received a greater harvest than he and his fishing partners could gather. It will be the same with us when we give obediently in thanksgiving to our Source and Sustainer—we'll be blessed beyond measure.

When you obey God, He promises you the following:

- He will set you high above all nations of the earth and give you favor that will distinguish you from others. (See Deuteronomy 28:1.)

- You will be blessed in the city and in the country, both in producing and in selling your goods. The *"fruit of your body"* (your children) will also be blessed and thereby return blessings to you, since they continue the work God has given to you. Moreover, you will be blessed by the produce of your ground; the increase of your herds, your cattle, and the offspring of your flocks; your basket; and your kneading bowl. In other words, you will have great success in all you do. (See verses 3–5, 11.)

- You will be blessed going out and coming in, no matter where. (See verse 6.)

- All your enemies will be defeated. You win! (See verse 7.)

- Your storehouses will be blessed. This promise applies to all of your resources and investments, which will increase in value. (See verse 8.)

- You will be established as holy unto God, and the nations will fear you. The world will know that you belong to God and that the only way they can succeed is by blessing you. (See verses 9–10.)

- The windows of heaven will open up and give you rain for your land in its season. God will bless all the work of your hand, increase your business and resources, and provide for you in the seasons when you need it most. (See verse 12.)

- You will lend and not borrow; you will be the head and not the tail, above and not beneath. This promise assures you of prosperity, blessings at work, never being in debt, leadership within your industry, and a state of continual increase. (See verse 13.)

Bringing In the Blessings

God's provision and protection enter your life in response to your obedience. When you obey God by tithing, He opens the windows of heaven (see Malachi 3:10), so that His blessings come directly to you. What does obedience look like, you ask? It's simpler than you might think: tithe, even when doing so might seem "unwise" in the eyes of the world.

Years ago, when my family was torn apart and everything was lost, I went to my accountant. He examined my finances carefully, turned to me, and said, "You need to stop tithing and giving all these offerings. You should also plan on filing bankruptcy."

I said, "Thank you very much," and then I walked out of his office. I immediately cut off those negative words and promptly hired a new accountant who agreed with the Word of God. As I continued to give faithfully, God supplied all my needs.

Supernatural Deliveries to My Daughter

When my daughter needed a car, she prayed with her husband about it. Because she was going to school, their budget was totally dependent on his income. In order to cut back, she proposed, "We could decrease our missions giving."

He immediately replied, "We will cut back on our food budget before we give up our missions giving." She agreed.

Two days later, they received a check in the mail for the amount of $1,000. "Surprises" such as this became a regular occurrence and ended up being a significant boost to their income while she finished her education. They remained faithful in their giving, and God blessed my daughter with a car.

Then, their new baby boy needed diapers. Instead of Daddy getting a second job, God supplied. Cases and cases of diapers were dropped off at their doorstep. There were enough diapers for the time he needed to wear them, as well as for his sisters when they came along! God is truly *able to do exceedingly abundantly above all that we ask or think"* (Ephesians 3:20).

If my daughter and son-in-law had cut back on their missions giving, that check would never have been delivered in the mail, and the other blessings would not have arrived!

A Natural Disaster Sparks Supernatural Blessings

After the January 2010 earthquake in Haiti, I traveled to the capital city, Port-au-Prince. The unemployment rate there was close to 90 percent. The earthquake had orphaned 500,000, killed 230,000, and left 300,000 injured. As many as 300,000 buildings had been destroyed, including most of the government buildings. In the capital city alone, over one million people lived in tents erected on top of the rubble in the medians between major avenues.

Sanitation was dependent on portable toilets provided by the United Nations. The underground water reservoirs were tainted, so bottled water was the only safe drinking water. Haiti was and still is in a desperate situation. But—praise God!—I led two days of pastoral training and three massive healing services. On one afternoon, I stressed the importance of tithing, yet the host pastor and I had previously agreed not to collect any offerings during the trip.

God had other plans, however. During my message, someone came forward and threw a few coins onto the stage. Another person did the same. More and more people came forward to put a few coins on the stage. Even though most of these individuals had only a few cents left, they believed God's Word and willingly gave what they had.

And God responded! Within the next few days, some of these faithful people received job offers. One man received a phone call regarding a teaching position at a university. Over the following weeks, we received numerous testimonies of healings and instances of God's divine financial provision for those who had obeyed His Word.

A Radical Turnaround in Ukraine

A number of years ago, my parents, Charles and Frances Hunter, held a healing school in the Ukraine when that nation was experiencing severe economic depression. Most of the people who attended the classes were quite poor.

My parents taught on the importance of tithes and offerings in relation to the release of God's financial blessings. The people responded with great enthusiasm. When Mom and Dad returned to Ukraine a year later, the team brought as many clothes as possible to give away to the poor.

When they arrived at the church, they were amazed at the transformation in the people. Most of the Ukrainians were dressed better than the American team members. And many of these team members took their "giveaway" clothes back home with them. A large number of the Ukrainians were driving their own cars. Of course, Mom and Dad wanted to know what had caused the dramatic change in these people's lives.

They found out that the people had responded to the teaching from the previous year by tithing faithfully and giving offerings, and that, when they had started this discipline, God had begun to bless them with prosperity. The people in this church had experienced a dramatic financial transformation in only one year, thanks to their obedience to God's Word!

The Curses of Disobedience

Just as there are blessings when we obey God, there are negative consequences when we disobey. These consequences are not to be taken lightly or ignored.

Malachi 3:10 tells us that the act of tithing opens the windows of heaven. Have you ever wondered what happens if you do not tithe? When we disobey, the exact opposite occurs. Disobeying God closes the windows of heaven. Rebellion against God's direction locks them shut.

Deuteronomy 28:15–68 warns us about the specific consequences of disobedience—fifty-four verses of curses! For each of the blessings of obedience, there is a corresponding curse for disobedience.

If you disobey God, the following curses may come upon you and overtake you:

- Cursing, confusion, and rebuke in all that you do until you are destroyed and perish quickly. (See Deuteronomy 28:20.)

- The plague will cling to you until it has consumed you, and you will not enter into your "Promised Land" (i.e., you will neither attain nor enjoy God's plans for your life). (See verses 21–22.)

- The earth and sky will not be conducive to whatever work you set out to do (i.e., success will be extremely difficult to attain); you will work hard but profit little. (See verses 23, 37–40, 42.)

- Anything that might have been a blessing, such as rain for your crops, will turn into a curse and work against you. (See verse 24.)

- Your enemies will defeat you. (See verse 25.)

- You will develop incurable boils, tumors, scabs, itches, and so forth. (See verses 27, 35, 59–61.)

- You will experience madness, blindness, and confusion of heart. (See verse 28.)

- You will not prosper; others will take advantage of you and steal from you. (See verse 29.)

- You will lose your spouse to another, and others will enjoy the fruit of your labors. (See verses 30–33, 41, 51.)

- Others will rise higher and higher above you as you fall lower and lower. (See verse 43.)

- You will borrow and not lend; you will be the tail and not the head. (See verse 44.)

- You will be made to serve your enemies, and they will treat you brutally; you will experience hunger, thirst, and nakedness; you will be in need of everything. (See verse 48.)

- Opposition, disrespect, dishonor, and complete destruction will come upon you. (See verses 49–57.)

- There will be extraordinary plagues and serious prolonged sicknesses for you and the generation that follows you. (See verses 59–61.)

- Lack and decrease will occur on all sides. (See verse 62.)

- You will be brought to nothing and plucked from the land. (See verse 63.)

- You will serve other gods. (See verses 36, 64.)

- You will find no place to rest and will suffer from a trembling heart, failing eyes, and anguish of soul. (See verse 65.)

- You will experience constant terror, anguish, and discontent. (See verses 66–67.)

You may wonder why I chose to list so many of the curses from Deuteronomy 28. After all, the "curses" passage isn't the type of Scripture you're likely to find in a devotional. You wouldn't select it as a reading on which to meditate as you start the day. Yet it's important to know what the Word of God says concerning our obedience—the good and the bad.

Perhaps you never realized that failing to tithe is an act of rebellion. Yet it's a decision to do the opposite of what God has instructed you to do. It is the same as your child not obeying your request to make his bed. Unfortunately, the consequences for not tithing are much more severe.

When you withhold your tithes and offerings, your life gets out of line. You may experience a loss of money elsewhere— for example, your car be damaged in an accident and need costly repairs, or you may be the victim of a robbery.

If you walk in obedience to God and listen to the Holy Spirit, the curses delineated in Deuteronomy 28 will not come upon you.

Maintain your focus on God and make His priorities your priorities. Tithe from the "firstfruits" of your increase, and He will supply all you need. If you walk in obedience to God and listen to the Holy Spirit, the curses delineated in Deuteronomy 28 will not come upon you. They become null and void. The Bible says several times that if you listen to and obey what God has commanded, disease and destruction will not come upon you.

> *Therefore you shall keep the commandment, the statutes, and the judgments which I command you today, to observe them. Then it shall come to pass, because you listen to these judgments, and keep and do them, that the LORD your God will keep with you the covenant and the mercy which He swore to your fathers. And He will love you and bless you and multiply you;... And the LORD will take away from you all sickness, and will afflict you with none of the terrible diseases of Egypt which you have known, but will lay them on all those who hate you.* (Deuteronomy 7:11–13, 15)

Follow Divine Promptings

The Holy Spirit is the One who speaks to you about giving. He is the One who quickens your spirit and makes your heart race just a little bit. He is your supernatural Guide for the natural steps you take in life, including where you direct your finances. The Holy Spirit will use divine nudges to prompt you to support certain missions organizations, outreaches, and ministries that need support.

He speaks to each person in His own way. Whether you are sitting in church or having lunch with friends, He can speak to you. He is not limited by your environment or conversation unless you have made Him unwelcome. When He speaks to you in that still, small voice, telling you what to give or how to help, it's up to you to obey. Follow His instructions, and He will continue to guide you because He knows you are a trustworthy servant.

Keys to Release Your Blessing

The blessings of God's kingdom do not come to everyone. There are keys that will show you how to align yourself with God's purposes so that you may release the blessings of Deuteronomy 28 into your life (and avoid the curses, as well).

Here are the most important keys that I have discovered:

Key #1: Repent

Repent of any foolish spending. Repent of the times you have failed to tithe. Repent of the occasions you refused to give an offering in obedience to God's direction. Confess that you have withheld your tithes and offerings because of a lack of faith.

Then, begin to give in faith, based on what the Holy Spirit has told you, not out of an emotional response or a guilt trip. Even when you think you cannot afford to give, God will tell you how much to give because He wants to bless you. Then, when the blessings start to pour into your life, you will know they are from Him.

Repeat this prayer aloud:

Father, I repent of all foolish spending. I confess that I have failed to tithe, and I repent of that, as well. I repent of any time I did not obey when You were prompting me to give an offering. I acknowledge those instances of disobedience as sin and ask that You would take that sin from me now and put it on the cross of Jesus Christ, never to be held against me again. Father, help me from this day forward to be careful about how I spend my money and to be faithful with the tithes and the offerings You tell me to give. In Jesus' name, amen.

Key #2: Refuse to Compromise

If the Holy Spirit directs you to give $100, and you give $25 with a mental promise to send the remaining $75 at a later date, you have just compromised. By this seemingly simple action, you have invited the curse of disobedience into your life.

In addition, if the Holy Spirit puts it on your heart to give $25, and you decide to give $100 instead, it is still disobedience. You are Jesus' sheep, and you know His voice. (See John 10:3–4, 16, 27.) So, regardless of what He tells you—how much to give, where to serve, or how to help—complete obedience should always be your response.

Key #3: Obey without Delay

It is not uncommon for believers to pray and ask God for a quick fix in any given situation. They pray boldly, ask Him to move on their behalf, and expect their "mountains" to disappear immediately. While His Word does tell us, *"Ask, and it will be given to you; seek, and you will find; knock, and it will be opened to you"* (Matthew 7:7), there's no guarantee that the results will come instantaneously. Yet many believers have the audacity to be impatient with God!

Let me ask you some questions. How fast do you respond when God asks you to do something? How quick are you to listen to the still, small voice of the Holy Spirit? How often do you obey completely the first time around? How long does God usually have to wait for you to obey Him?

Parents know the importance of immediate obedience. When a father tells his children to pick up their toys, make their beds, or finish their homework, he expects them to obey immediately (or in the very near future). If the children delay in fulfilling their father's request, it can be very frustrating for him. What makes you think your heavenly Father is any different?

When God asks you, His child, to do something, He expects you to respond by obeying His instructions the first time around, without grumbling and groaning. He does not enjoy the whines and complaints of His children any more than an earthly parent does.

> **God will never ask you to do something unless it will bless you and others.**

Remember that He is your heavenly Father, who wants only the best for you. He will never ask you to do something unless it will bless you and others.

Every good gift and every perfect gift is from above, and comes down from the Father of lights, with whom there is no variation or shadow of turning.

(James 1:17)

When you are walking in complete obedience, you are dwelling in the perfect will of God. It is impossible to do what God has called you to do unless you obey Him. Now that you know how important obedience is, you must make every effort to do all that God asks of you.

Is it always easy to be obedient? No. Sometimes, you simply have to stand in faith to do things God's way. Start with small steps, and your walk of obedience will become more and more natural.

Disobedience is the deadbolt on the windows of heaven. Practice obedience so that God may throw them open wide and pour out His blessings on you!

Q & A about Tithes, Offerings, and Alms

I sometimes receive e-mails with specific questions about tithes, offerings, and alms. As you seek to obey the Lord with your finances, you may have similar questions about the particulars of these areas. Therefore, I have included some representative questions here, as well as my responses, to further clarify these concepts and their implications.

"In the Old Testament, hungry people and priests benefited from tithed food. I understand that churches need money. What are some other instances of giving that would be considered tithing?"

—P. R.

My response: "Some people tithe off their crop or harvest. A farmer in our church in Dallas did this. He always tithed his first crop to the ministry. Obviously, he didn't bring in truckloads of wheat or corn to the church. He sold the produce and donated his profit to the work of the ministry as his tithe."

———————

"Let's say that you are an electrician, and the church hires you to do a job, but you don't accept payment for your services. Does this count as planting a seed? And does a donation of time and service count as a tithe or offering, or does planting a seed always involve giving money?"

—J. S.

My response: "It is good for everyone to give of his time and talents to his church or to a specific ministry. Those people without an abundance of money to give can tithe their time or their talents to meet the needs of God's people. God will bless these donations with His usual generosity. You can seed or give anything—time, prayer, food, and even advice."

———————

"How do we make a decision about where to tithe, and how much is right? Is there a minimum?"

—K. L.

My response: "The minimum tithe is 10 percent of your income, but whether you tithe off the gross or the net is up to you. I always tithe based on the gross amount, before any taxes or deductions have been taken out. Listen for God's direction and tithe accordingly.

"Many people believe the tithe needs to go to the local church. I believe the tithe needs to go where God tells you to give it. Often, it is the local church. On occasion, though, He may direct you to do something different. He may ask you to give the tithe where you are being spiritually fed. Who is your spiritual covering? To whom do you turn when you need someone to agree with you in prayer? Where do you go for spiritual consultation, mentoring, or counsel?"

"Is it considered tithing to give food when someone is hungry?"

—M. W.

My response: "No, unless you have nothing else to give. Giving food is often considered alms. Let me explain with a vivid example of almsgiving: I remember a story told to me by Evelyn Roberts, wife of evangelist Oral Roberts. A certain woman had sent her some cheese that she had received from the government food bank. Evelyn held that cheese and cried. She wanted to send it back. But God said to her, 'This cheese was all she had to give.' Evelyn prayed over the cheese and asked God to bless the woman for giving so sacrificially."

"I am currently involved in the local church. We have a new pastor. After a year, I am realizing more and more that I don't agree with much of her teaching. I don't think that she believes the Bible was truly inspired by God or the miracles in the Bible were anything more than bad weather and man's attempt to explain it. I doubt she even believes that Satan exists.

"I find myself missing church more and more, which also means I miss putting money in the offering basket, which I always understood was tithing. I have never tithed with regularity and only recently in the last year decided that I wanted to do it, but I am not all that thrilled with my church. I feel guilty not giving there because it is an old building that needs a new roof.

"My church needs all the offerings and tithes they can bring in to repair the building. I love the church community and I don't want to lose out on those friendships. What is a person to do? The building will only outlive the pastor if it is taken care of."

—D. C.

My response: "Give as God directs you to. He wants you to give in faith and obedience, not out of a sense of guilt or obligation. A minister may beg and plead for people to give toward one project or another. Listen to God's voice, not man's."

"I have received a large sum of money and I feel compelled to tithe, but where? How do I decide where to seed my money? Last year, a new pastor asked for money for a healing service. He said he needed $100. It was the largest amount I had ever given at one time. It was wonderful to give it to him for this purpose.

"Two weeks later, he died, and the service went on without him. I have no idea if the money was ever used for the service. Is that an example of wasting a tithe? I did not have a word from God before giving it, nor did I expect one. I only prayed and asked God to use it."

—H. B.

My response: "Just remember, you gave to God. No matter what the person did or didn't do with it, you gave it to Him. You have to trust that God used your money as He intended and will bless it back to you. At the time, you felt led to give by the Holy Spirit, and you acted in obedience."

"What do you do when you don't hear from God and the plate is being passed?"

—J. T.

My response: "God tells you what, where, and when to give when you are sensitive to His voice."

In order to open up the windows of heaven and activate the blessings of God, the one thing you need to do is give. Give something to God. Exercise your faith in His promises. Give to the local church that is feeding you. Give to a ministry that has "good soil." Give where God tells you to plant your seed. Practice obedience and reap His blessings!

Pray this prayer aloud:

Father, I confess that I haven't always obeyed You by giving my tithes, offerings, and alms, and I repent. You know what my need is, even better than I do. You also know better than the devil knows what I will do with the blessings that You will pour out upon me as a reward for my obedience.

Father, please tell me what to give and where. I know that You will take care of all my concerns and bless every corner of my life. In Jesus' name, amen.

Chapter 7

Provision Comes in Many Ways

If My people who are called by My name will humble themselves, and pray and seek My face, and turn from their wicked ways, then I will hear from heaven, and will forgive their sin and heal their land.
—2 Chronicles 7:14

The above promise of blessings from God sounds a lot like those from Deuteronomy 28 that we explored in the last chapter. In this particular verse, God tells His people that He will *"heal their land."*

I know that believers often get together to pray for their "land," meaning their nation, but God has shown me that *"land"* means so much more.

Now the LORD had said to Abram: "Get out of your country, from your family and from your father's house, to a land that I will show you. I will make you a great nation; I will bless you and make your name great; and you shall be a blessing. I will bless those who bless you, and I will curse him who curses you; and in you all the families of the earth shall be blessed." (Genesis 12:1–3)

Yes, the Lord promised physical land to Abraham and his descendants in Genesis 12, but the blessings He had in mind were far greater than a piece of property.

What is your "land"? I believe the land God has for you to possess includes health and well-being for your body, your home, your transportation, your job, your family—everything that pertains to you and your life! Think of it as something very personal.

Recognize Your Riches

And God raised us up with Christ and seated us with him in the heavenly realms in Christ Jesus, in order that in the coming ages he might show the incomparable riches of his grace, expressed in his kindness to us in Christ Jesus. (Ephesians 2:6–7 NIV)

Even though much of this book discusses how God prospers us through the multiplication of our finances, His supernatural provision is not limited to cash. His blessings go far beyond the money that passes through your hands or collects in your bank account.

Beloved, I pray that you may prosper in all things and be in health, just as your soul prospers. (3 John 2)

Divine prosperity includes but is not limited to life, love, health, hope, and wealth. Your heavenly Father wants you to prosper in all areas of your life—not only in your finances but also in your body, soul, mind, spirit, relationships, and so forth.

Your heavenly Father wants you to prosper in all areas of your life—not only in your finances.

We have the opportunity every day to thank God for every breath we take, the food we eat, the clothes we wear, our spouses, our families, our children, our jobs, and our health. Everything we enjoy is a blessing from God.

Yes, God receives the money we give to Him and often multiplies it back in cash; however, His blessings may take a completely different form. Do you recognize and acknowledge the many intangible blessings that exceed your taxable income?

God is very creative in the ways He blesses us. No matter how His blessings arrive, remember that you are blessed to be a blessing, not to hoard the blessings for yourself. Again, God wants you to have nice "things," as long as those things do not have you.

As you read through the rest of this chapter, seek to recognize the ways in which God has blessed you that do not specifically involve money. Then, create a personal "Blessing List" to acknowledge His supernatural provision in your life. For instance, has someone taken you out for dinner? Has a neighbor given your child a bicycle that her kids no longer use? Have you found an excellent sale on something you need? All of these are blessings that increase your overall net worth.

Prospering in the Midst of Adversity

Disasters happen. The enemy attacks at unexpected moments to derail or distract you from God's ultimate plans.

Again, you have a choice. Do you recognize the source of the attack, or do you sink into self-pity and depression? God can take any situation and turn it into a blessing—an instance of divine provision—if only you will keep your eyes open to recognize it as such. Allow me to share an example from a good friend of mine who acknowledged God's provision in the midst of a devastating situation.

"Normally, I am asleep by 11:30 or 12:00 at night. On this particular evening, I was checking one more thing online before turning out the lights. Suddenly, I heard an unfamiliar sound. As I walked toward my office, I noticed a strange light in the loft of my home. The dogs were in their beds downstairs, so I knew they were not the source of the strange noise I had heard.

"I climbed the stairs to the loft, wondering what could be happening. I had had a candle burning in my loft for twelve years, but I always used a protective device to prevent accidental fires and kept nothing flammable nearby. In fact, the electricity didn't even work in that area of my home. I would spend hours reading the Bible or praying in this special "prayer closet" in my home.

"When I saw that the small table was on fire, I ran to the bathroom, grabbed a wastebasket, filled it with water, and rushed back to the loft. I poured the water over the fire. But instead of dousing the flames, the water literally exploded the fire. Black smoke billowed up toward the ceiling and over the balcony into the rest of the house. Sparks landed on both of my hands and my foot, as well as the hem of the caftan I was wearing.

"Realizing that I wouldn't be able to control the flames, I ran downstairs and grabbed the house phone to call for help. The 9-1-1 responder asked the usual questions and then told me firmly to exit the house immediately. I had fully intended to get my fire extinguisher from the kitchen and return to the loft, but the woman was adamant that I get the dogs and myself out of the house without further delay. So, I released my dogs to run loose on the back patio and then ran in the other direction, toward the front door, still talking on the phone to the 9-1-1 responder.

"Barefoot, I ran out the door and traveled about five feet when the window in the loft exploded, showering shards of glass behind me as I ran. If I had been ten seconds behind, I would have been running over broken glass.

"When the fire trucks arrived, the flames were licking their way up through the loft window and onto the roof as black smoke rolled throughout the rest of the structure. I stood on the cold street, watching the firefighters aim a water hose through the broken window into my home, and several of my neighbors gathered with me. Police cars and an ambulance arrived with sirens blaring and lights flashing.

"It was a surreal scene. I was in shock, but my anger flared when I recognized the source of this attack: Satan himself. I started binding him by proclaiming, 'Satan, you tried, but you lose!' Then, I praised God and said, 'God is taking care of me. God, take it all, if You wish. It's all small stuff. You have renewed and restored me before, and You will do it again!'

> I praised God and said, "God is taking care of me. God, take it all, if You wish. It's all small stuff. You have renewed and restored me before, and You will do it again!"

"After three hours of chaos, the firefighters allowed me to reenter my house, though I was not permitted to take anything out of the house. I walked across the waterlogged carpet, surveying the mess with the dim beam of a flashlight.

I grabbed my laptop, my Bible, and my very unhappy dogs and left my beautiful home. My daughter and son-in-law had been contacted by the police and had come over to take me and my nervous animals to the safety of their home.

"I was sitting on the bed, trying to sort out the events of the evening, when my daughter brought me some of her clothes to wear. I had never been able to fit into my daughter's clothes; she has always been slim and trim. But, because I had recently lost 100 pounds, I was able to fit into her clothes! And, for the first time that night, I actually smiled.

"For the next three nights, I lay awake and stared at the ceiling for hours at a time while thanking God for His protection. I even thanked Him for the simple ability to lie there and watch the ceiling fan go around and around and around all night long. I could still breathe. I could still feel. I was still alive!

"I went back to the house every day and watched complete strangers from the restoration company pack up my belongings. It was not pleasant knowing that it was up to others to decide what was salvageable and what needed to be thrown away. I forced myself to watch and accept the possibility that I would have nothing left.

"The fire destroyed most of the loft, including the roof. The damage to the rest of my home was caused primarily by the smoke and soot, which permeated nearly everything. Because of the carcinogenic properties of the soot, everything had to be professionally cleaned. The air conditioner had spread the contaminated air throughout the house, and the heat had destroyed the ductwork in the attic, as well as the air-conditioning unit.

"The insurance company rented a home for me and contacted me regularly to make sure they were meeting my needs. I was not fussy about temporary housing. My concern was having a place conducive to my pets' comfort rather than my own. I would survive. I knew how to 'camp.' Indeed, my 'camping' lasted four-and-a-half months. My frequent visits to my home were bittersweet as I watched the workers gut my house and restore it piece by piece.

"When the restoration work was nearly finished, I purchased new appliances for the kitchen. Two days after they were delivered, they were stolen. But I refused to be defeated! Back to the store I went to buy another set.

"When moving day finally arrived, my furniture arrived from one side of town, while the rest of my belongings were delivered from the other direction. Boxes were scattered throughout my house, with identification labels that were not at all detailed, which meant that every box I opened was like a Christmas surprise. I may never know exactly what I lost, but I do know what I found.

"God was faithful in so many ways! He had kept me awake on the night of the fire. If I had been asleep, I never would have gotten out of the house alive. The smoke would have trapped me in my bedroom. Today, I am alive to serve Him, and I thank Him for both spiritual and physical salvation.

> **Today, I am alive to serve God, and I thank Him for both spiritual and physical salvation.**

"Three days after the fire, I had received a phone call informing me that I had been selected for a special honor in a national organization to which I belong. Not knowing whether to cry or to smile, I did a little of both at the same time. I truly had God's favor during a very difficult time.

"My home is now restored. It is not exactly the way it was before—it's better! I had replaced the roof, siding, windows, and foundation years prior to the fire. The interior needed work, but I hadn't been able to start any major renovations or improvements. By the time this 'adventure' was over, the insurance company had invested $140,000 into my life. When I found out the total, my first thought was, *How can I possibly tithe on that amount?*

"This was not the first miracle God has showered on me, and I know it will not be the last, either. He is so good! Truly, what Satan intended for utter disaster in my life, God turned into a total miracle. It is now a great testimony to His faithfulness, goodness, and love for one of His kids!"

What a testimony! My friend was able to recognize God's miraculous provision in the midst of what most people would see as a complete disaster. How has the Lord blessed you in spite of dire circumstances? Do your own Bible study on His blessings. You will receive your own personal revelation of endless blessings as you read and discover what God has provided for your eyes only. Pray that God will open your ears and that the scales will fall from your eyes as His revelations come forth through His Holy Spirit. You will find other verses that apply. Listening to Christian radio or TV, you will be reminded of other ways He is blessing you. Suddenly, you will realize that the *"riches of his grace"* (Ephesians 2:7 NIV) surround you every day.

Just experiencing everyday life with open spiritual eyes will show you the many ways in which God has blessed you, provided for your needs, and protected you from the attacks of the enemy.

Make a "Blessing List"

Start your "Blessing List" today. List the blessings God has already given to you and those you love. He gives you every breath you breathe, every beat of your heart. Keep thanking and praising Him! He gives only good gifts, and He'll never stop! He loves you!

What has God done for you today? What has He done for your family? What has He done for your church? Remember, He cares about the little things, so include those on your list, too.

He may not immediately drop provision at your feet when you think it should appear. However, know that He will always supply in His perfect timing.

To help you with your "Blessings List," here is a sampling of scriptural promises, but it's by no means exhaustive.

The Desires of Your Heart

Do not fret because of evildoers, nor be envious of the workers of iniquity....Trust in the LORD, and do good; dwell in the land, and feed on His faithfulness. Delight yourself also in the LORD, and He shall give you the desires of your heart. Commit your way to the LORD, trust also in Him, and He shall bring it to pass....Rest in the LORD, and wait patiently for Him.
(Psalm 37:1, 3–5, 7)

Enjoyment of the Fruits of Your Labor

...that every man should eat and drink and enjoy the good of all his labor...is the gift of God.
(Ecclesiastes 3:13)

It is good and fitting for one to eat and drink, and to enjoy the good of all his labor in which he toils under the sun all the days of his life which God gives him; for it is his heritage. As for every man to whom God has given riches and wealth, and given him power to eat of it, to receive his heritage and rejoice in his labor—this is the gift of God.   (Ecclesiastes 5:18–19)

Favor

For You, O LORD, will bless the righteous; with favor You will surround him as with a shield.

(Psalm 5:12)

For His anger is but for a moment, His favor is for life; weeping may endure for a night, but joy comes in the morning.   (Psalm 30:5)

My son, do not forget my law, but let your heart keep my commands; for length of days and long life and peace they will add to you. Let not mercy and truth forsake you; bind them around your neck, write them on the tablet of your heart, and so find favor and high esteem in the sight of God and man.

(Proverbs 3:1–4)

For whoever finds me [wisdom] *finds life, and obtains favor from the LORD.*   (Proverbs 8:35)

An End-Time Harvest

(God has plans to finance the end-time harvest. I believe there will be a miraculous money transfer from the sinner to the righteous, from the disobedient to the obedient.)

A good man leaves an inheritance to his children's children, but the wealth of the sinner is stored up for the righteous.   (Proverbs 13:22)

...but to the sinner [God] *gives the work of gathering and collecting, that he may give to him who is good before God.* (Ecclesiastes 2:26)

Health and Healing

Many are the afflictions of the righteous, but the LORD delivers him out of them all. He guards all his bones; not one of them is broken. (Psalm 34:19–20)

Bless the LORD, O my soul, and forget not all His benefits: who forgives all your iniquities, who heals all your diseases. (Psalm 103:2–3)

Surely [Jesus] *took up our infirmities and carried our sorrows, yet we considered him stricken by God, smitten by him, and afflicted. But he was pierced for our transgressions, he was crushed for our iniquities; the punishment that brought us peace was upon him, and by his wounds we are healed.* (Isaiah 53:4–5 NIV)

Land, Inheritance, and Descendants

But I said to you, "You will possess their land; I will give it to you as an inheritance, a land flowing with milk and honey." I am the LORD your God, who has set you apart from the nations. (Leviticus 20:24 NIV)

Then the LORD your God will bring you to the land which your fathers possessed, and you shall possess it. He will prosper you and multiply you more than your fathers. (Deuteronomy 30:5)

I command you today to love the Lord your God, to walk in His ways, and to keep His commandments, His statutes, and His judgments, that you may live and multiply; and the Lord your God will bless you in the land which you go to possess. (Deuteronomy 30:16)

The Lord has been mindful of us; He will bless us; He will bless the house of Israel; He will bless the house of Aaron. He will bless those who fear the Lord, both small and great. May the Lord give you increase more and more, you and your children. May you be blessed by the Lord, who made heaven and earth. (Psalm 115:12–15)

Peace, Rest, and Assurance

These things I have spoken to you, that in Me you may have peace. In the world you will have tribulation; but be of good cheer, I have overcome the world. (John 16:33)

You will keep him in perfect peace, whose mind is stayed on You, because he trusts in You. (Isaiah 26:3)

Come to Me, all you who labor and are heavy laden, and I will give you rest. Take My yoke upon you and learn from Me, for I am gentle and lowly in heart, and you will find rest for your souls. For My yoke is easy and My burden is light. (Matthew 11:28–30)

And He said, "My Presence will go with you, and I will give you rest." (Exodus 33:14)

Peace I leave with you, My peace I give to you; not as the world gives do I give to you. Let not your heart be troubled, neither let it be afraid. (John 14:27)

Protection

*Then they cried out to the L*ORD *in their trouble, and He saved them out of their distresses.* (Psalm 107:19)

*Let all those rejoice who put their trust in You; let them ever shout for joy, because You defend them; let those also who love Your name be joyful in You. For You, O L*ORD*, will bless the righteous; with favor You will surround him as with a shield.* (Psalm 5:11–12)

*The L*ORD *is my rock, my fortress and my deliverer; my God is my rock, in whom I take refuge, my shield and the horn of my salvation. He is my stronghold, my refuge and my savior—from violent men you save me. I call to the L*ORD*, who is worthy of praise, and I am saved from my enemies.*

(2 Samuel 22:2–4 NIV)

Eternal Rewards

Blessed are the poor in spirit, for theirs is the kingdom of heaven. Blessed are those who mourn, for they shall be comforted. Blessed are the meek, for they shall inherit the earth. Blessed are those who hunger and thirst for righteousness, for they shall be filled. Blessed are the merciful, for they shall obtain mercy. Blessed are the pure in heart, for they shall see God. Blessed are the peacemakers, for they shall be called sons of God. Blessed are those who are persecuted for righteousness' sake, for theirs is the kingdom of heaven. (Matthew 5:3–10)

And they sang a new song, saying: "You are worthy to take the scroll, and to open its seals; for You were slain, and have redeemed us to God by Your blood out of every tribe and tongue and people and nation, and have made us kings and priests to our God; and we shall reign on the earth." (Revelation 5:9–10)

Success in All You Do

You shall surely give to [the poor], *and your heart should not be grieved when you give to* [them], *because for this thing the LORD your God will bless you in all your works and in all to which you put your hand.* (Deuteronomy 15:10)

This Book of the Law shall not depart from your mouth, but you shall meditate in it day and night, that you may observe to do according to all that is written in it. For then you will make your way prosperous, and then you will have good success. (Joshua 1:8)

And I will give you treasures hidden in the darkness—secret riches. I will do this so you may know that I am the LORD, the God of Israel, the one who calls you by name. (Isaiah 45:3 NLT)

For I will look on you favorably and make you fruitful, multiply you and confirm My covenant with you. (Leviticus 26:9)

And I will multiply the fruit of your trees and the increase of your fields, so that you need never again bear the reproach of famine among the nations.
(Ezekiel 36:30)

The LORD your God will make you abound in all the work of your hand, in the fruit of your body, in the increase of your livestock, and in the produce of your land for good. For the LORD will again rejoice over you for good as He rejoiced over your fathers.
(Deuteronomy 30:9)

The righteous shall flourish like a palm tree, he shall grow like a cedar in Lebanon. (Psalm 92:12)

Blessed is the man who trusts in the LORD, and whose hope is the LORD. For he shall be like a tree planted by the waters, which spreads out its roots by the river, and will not fear when heat comes; but its leaf will be green, and will not be anxious in the year of drought, nor will cease from yielding fruit.
(Jeremiah 17:7–8)

Blessed is the man who walks not in the counsel of the ungodly, nor stands in the path of sinners, nor sits in the seat of the scornful; but his delight is in the law of the LORD, and in His law he meditates day and night....And whatever he does shall prosper.
(Psalm 1:1–2, 3)

And keep the charge of the LORD your God: to walk in His ways, to keep His statutes, His commandments, His judgments, and His testimonies, as it is written in the Law of Moses, that you may prosper in all that you do and wherever you turn. (1 Kings 2:3)

Wisdom and Knowledge

For God gives wisdom and knowledge and joy to a man who is good in His sight. (Ecclesiastes 2:26)

I will certainly give you the wisdom and knowledge you requested. (2 Chronicles 1:12 NLT)

Blessed is the man who finds wisdom, the man who gains understanding, for she is more profitable than silver and yields better returns than gold. She is more precious than rubies; nothing you desire can compare with her. Long life is in her right hand; in her left hand are riches and honor. Her ways are pleasant ways, and all her paths are peace. (Proverbs 3:13–17 NIV)

I, wisdom, dwell with prudence, and find out knowledge and discretion....Counsel is mine, and sound wisdom; I am understanding, I have strength....I love those who love me, and those who seek me diligently will find me. Riches and honor are with me, enduring riches and righteousness. My fruit is better than gold, yes, than fine gold, and my revenue than choice silver. I traverse the way of righteousness, in the midst of the paths of justice, that I may cause those who love me to inherit wealth, that I may fill their treasuries. (Proverbs 8:12, 14, 17–21)

Through wisdom a house is built, and by understanding it is established; by knowledge the rooms

are filled with all precious and pleasant riches.
(Proverbs 24:3–4)

The Words to Speak

Then the Lord reached out his hand and touched my mouth and said to me, "Now, I have put my words in your mouth." (Jeremiah 1:9 NIV)

And then I'll stir up fresh hope in Israel—the dawn of deliverance!—and I'll give you, Ezekiel, bold and confident words to speak. And they'll realize that I am God. (Ezekiel 29:21 MSG)

Now when they bring you to the synagogues and magistrates and authorities, do not worry about how or what you should answer, or what you should say. For the Holy Spirit will teach you in that very hour what you ought to say. (Luke 12:11–12)

Chapter 8

Claim Your Inheritance

The Spirit Himself bears witness with our spirit
that we are children of God, and if children, then
heirs; heirs of God and joint heirs with Christ.
—Romans 8:16–17

Several years ago, I was at the bank when I encountered a small, elderly lady who had just finished her business and appeared totally drained and burdened with sorrow.

I approached her and said, "May I pray with you? May I give you a hug?"

She said yes, and so I gave her a hug. She then asked me for a ride home, and I agreed to take her. In the car, she said, "You're so sweet, honey. I know you don't have any idea what it means to be betrayed."

She looked a bit surprised when I said, "Yes, I do. I even wrote a book about what happened to me." I had a copy of my book *Healing the Heart* in the car, so I gave it to her.

She told me that her husband had died seven years prior. They had lived in a very nice home, but she had lost everything after he died. Only two weeks earlier, she had discovered that her husband had died a multimillionaire. Meanwhile, ever since his death, she had been living below the poverty line. The executor of her husband's will had withheld all of her inheritance and given it to her husband's business partner and best friend, instead.

What a tragic story of injustice! This woman's inheritance was illegally withheld from her. I tell you this story because I want to ask you this question: Who is holding back your inheritance?

Your inheritance is the anointing of the Holy Spirit, the power of the blood of Jesus over evil, peace that passes understanding, and an abundant life. All of your needs are met in Christ Jesus. This is your inheritance, already given to you, and it is a tragedy to suffer the injustice of it being withheld from you!

You have to reach the point where you are not going to put up with it anymore. You have had enough. The enemy— *"the thief* [who] *does not come except to steal, and to kill, and to destroy"* (John 10:10)—has taken more than you should have to bear. It is past time for restoration and life. Kick the enemy out of your life and finances. When difficult situations come against me, I say, "Satan, you are trespassing, and you must leave, in Jesus' name."

Blessing Blockers

Sometimes, however, we miss out on our inheritance because of our own sins and shortcomings. Let's discuss some of the major roadblocks to receiving our inheritance and how we can overcome them.

Doubt

This almost goes without saying, but we must not doubt God's ability to meet our needs—and even to exceed them. A good example of someone who was rewarded for unwavering faith is the widow in this account from 2 Kings:

> *A certain woman of the wives of the sons of the prophets cried out to Elisha, saying, "Your servant my husband is dead, and you know that your servant feared the LORD. And the creditor is coming to take my two sons to be his slaves." So Elisha said to her, "What shall I do for you? Tell me, what do you have in the house?" And she said, "Your maidservant has nothing in the house but a jar of oil." Then he said, "Go, borrow vessels from everywhere, from all your neighbors; empty vessels; do not gather just a few. And when you have come in, you shall shut the door behind you and your sons; then pour it into all those vessels, and set aside the full ones." So she went from him and shut the door behind her and her sons, who brought the vessels to her; and she poured it out. Now it came to pass, when the vessels were full, that she said to her son, "Bring me another vessel." And he said to her, "There is not another vessel." So the oil ceased. Then she came and told the man of God. And he said, "Go, sell the oil and pay your debt; and you and your sons live on the rest."*   (verses 1–7)

Had the widow doubted Elisha's God-given instructions and ignored them, her oil would not have multiplied supernaturally, and she would not have been able to pay her debt. But, because she obeyed in faith, she received a blessing—one that she alone had the power to limit, based on the number of vessels she managed to borrow. If she had borrowed more containers, she would have been blessed even more.

Never doubt God's ability or desire to bless you. He knows exactly where, when, and how the money you need will arrive. Raise your level of anticipation, and do not question His methods, even if they do not align with your expectations.

Pride

Life's twists and turns may sometimes prove more of an uphill battle than you anticipated. In those times, you might pray and ask God to move on your behalf. You might beg and plead with Him to move a mountain into the sea. Or, you might stand on Scripture and believe that God will supply the money for a mortgage payment, for example. But you might not expect Him to get the finances to you in the way that He chooses to.

For the LORD God is a sun and shield; the LORD will give grace and glory; no good thing will He withhold from those who walk uprightly. (Psalm 84:11)

God can move on anyone, anytime, anywhere, to bless you!

When you trust God to meet a need, you have to understand that He often works through other people to supply the finances you have been praying for. He can move on anyone, anytime, anywhere, to bless you!

Sometimes, we miss out on these blessings because of pride. I know a couple with two daughters. When the girls were nine and ten years of age, their parents set long-term goals for the girls' education and believed that God would supernaturally fund their college tuitions.

One day, one of the wife's coworkers came to her and said, "My mom just died and left me millions of dollars. I would like to set your children up with a college fund, if for no other reason than for the tax deduction."

She said, "Let me go check with my husband."

But when she told him about the woman's desire to set up a college fund for their daughters, her husband said, "No, I'm not taking any of her money. I am going to do it on my own."

God wanted to bless this couple and their children, but pride blocked the blessing! Be willing to receive blessings from others. Be thankful when people around you have seen your need and offer their help. Do not let pride keep you from accepting a gift.

God is trying to get money to you. Don't ever say, "No! I'll do it myself." Reach out and receive!

Compromise

Several years ago, my daughter Melody was signed up with an organization that did overseas missions work with orphans. One particular trip she wanted to make would entail going to Russia and Romania for one month. She needed to raise $3,500 to cover her cost of the trip. Many people contributed money to help pay her way. However, two weeks before the deadline, she still needed $1,200. She had contributed a lot of her salary, as well as participated in various fund-raisers, to reach her goal.

Facing this seemingly unreachable goal with the deadline fast approaching, she called her dad (my ex-husband) to ask him to help pay for the trip. Since he had not yet given any money for that purpose, she thought he might be willing to help her.

It turns out that he was not willing to give money, but he did suggest another solution: "Why don't you come and speak at my church next Sunday and tell everyone where you are going and what you are doing?" he said. "Bring pictures from your last trip and tell the congregation what your need is, and we'll receive an offering for your trip. How does that sound?"

Sounds good, right? There were just a few problems with his offer. Melody's dad pastors a church where most of the members lead an alternative lifestyle. Melody had never been to the church or attended a service there because of her position that this alternative lifestyle is not scriptural.

There was no guarantee that the money she needed for her trip would arrive before the deadline. She could have compromised her standards and taken this opportunity to try to raise the money she needed, but the Holy Spirit spoke to her heart, "This is not the best idea."

Disappointed and a little frustrated, Melody told her dad, "I'll think about it." She needed to pray about the opportunity that her father had presented. She chose to believe that God was going to provide through a different source. She called her pastor, explained the situation, and asked for wisdom and guidance. He did not answer immediately but assured her that he would consider the options and let her know what he felt God wanted her to do in the situation.

Melody ultimately declined her father's offer to speak at his church. A few days before the deadline for making her final trip payment, Melody was sitting with the team in the last meeting they would have before departure. In the middle of the meeting, her phone rang. It was her pastor calling to tell her the church was giving her $1,000 toward the missions trip! She ultimately received everything she needed to go to Russia and Romania.

She had not compromised. She had not questioned God or panicked during the long hours of waiting for Him to work out the final details. She knew that speaking at a church that sanctions an alternate lifestyle would have been a compromise that would have altered her future and weakened her witness. God has miraculously supplied her need on many occasions since then, and she freely shares her testimony about her great God with everyone she meets.

The Acceptance of Questionable Gifts

Sometimes, receiving is easy. We glorify God with thankfulness and excitement. Other times, though, as soon as we receive something, whether it's a gift or some money, our stress level rises. And this is not necessarily a bad thing.

The Holy Spirit can make you feel uneasy about receiving a gift for different reasons. He may be warning you about the heart motives of the person who offers you the gift. He knows when someone gives out of a generous heart or a greedy, self-seeking spirit.

God may be warning you about the heart motives of the person who offers you the gift. He knows when someone gives out of a generous heart or a greedy, self-seeking spirit.

For example, when finances are offered with accompanying conditions to a friend or relative, it is often difficult for that friend or relative to receive the assistance. It is one thing to give money and say, "This is for your electric bill" and expect the person to pay his bill. That condition is acceptable because the need is the electric bill. But to say, "Here is some money. Don't use it for getting coffee or going out. You can have it only if you agree to use it on such-and-such" tends to put the recipient in an awkward position and may pressure him to compromise his standards.

Someone who gives with conditions might say something like, "I'll buy your dinner if you come visit me." If something is offered with strings attached, or if accepting it would require you to compromise your beliefs, ask the Holy Spirit for guidance. You may get your bills paid, but the strain on your relationship with someone and the trapped feeling that accompanies indebtedness may not be worth what you receive in the long run.

There can be some exceptions to this general wisdom about not accepting money with conditions attached. When one of my daughters graduated from college, a family member said, "I'm so proud of you! Here is some graduation money. Spend it on whatever you like, just don't buy a car." It wasn't enough to buy a car, but it was enough to make a sizable down payment. My daughter needed a car, and she decided that it was her money to spend however she chose.

So, she bought a car. You may be thinking, *It was her need, it was her money, and she was an adult. That person didn't have the right to tell her how to spend the gift.*

Yet, by the time my daughter had finished paying for the car, she was beyond ready to get rid of it! She nearly hated it. She disliked spending money on that car—regular maintenance fees, oil changes, new tires, and so forth. When she received the money as a graduation gift, she ignored the wisdom that was offered at the same time. Occasionally, accepting a gift with conditions and then contravening them can bring a curse.

Sometimes, "gifts" are given in the form of a loan, on the condition that the recipient eventually repay with interest. Romans 13:8 instructs us to *"let no debt remain outstanding, except the continuing debt to love one another"* (NIV).

God knows the awkwardness that arises when one family member has loaned money to another and has not been paid back. He wants us to avoid borrowing from one another. If a family member is in need, and you have money to spare, consider giving it to him or her as a gift rather than a loan. Pray and ask God if you should supply their need.

In Luke 6:38, Jesus said, *"Give, and it will be given to you: good measure, pressed down, shaken together, and running over will be put into your bosom. For with the same measure that you use, it will be measured back to you."* I would rather give freely to my relatives in need and look to God to multiply the amount back to me with good measure, pressed down and shaken together, than to give them loans and then look at them in frustration, wanting to press them down and shake them together to force the payments plus interest out of them!

How do you know when you should receive gifts of any kind from people around you? It is best to receive a gift when it is offered to you freely, without conditions. God freely gives salvation and forgiveness. You cannot do anything to earn them. Jesus freely died on the cross for your salvation and took the punishment for your sins. His death gave you the provision for forgiveness. It is a debt you cannot repay.

It is best to receive a gift when it is offered to you freely, without conditions.

Another appropriate time to receive a gift from someone is when it is a specific answer to a need or prayer, even if the answer comes through a relative. As long as the gift stays free of unreasonable conditions or compromise, thank God for your relative's generosity.

A couple of years ago, my daughter Melody was praying and believing God for a laptop. She was working for me and had started traveling with the ministry team to help on the road. In order to get the laptop with the "friends and family" discount at a particular store, she needed to order it within two weeks.

To come up with the necessary $1,000 in two weeks was unrealistic in the natural. Melody was traveling with me at the time, and God put it on her heart to give $100 to our ministry. She went back and forth with God for a few minutes, explaining to Him that she was just helping and did not have any finances coming in while she was on the road with me. But, in her heart, she knew she had heard God and gave the money out of obedience.

Two days later, I received a phone call. The person on the other end of the phone said, "I believe God told me to give Melody $1,000. Is that okay?"

I paused for a second and then said, "Yes." That person had no idea that Melody had been praying and believing for that exact amount of money to purchase a laptop. With no strings attached, without any guidelines as to how Melody was to use the $1,000, that person gave freely.

While it is crucial to evaluate the motives of the gift giver before you accept a gift, it is equally important to know your own motives before you ask for something from God or from another person. Keep in mind James 4:3: *"When you ask, you do not receive, because you ask with wrong motives, that you may spend what you get on your pleasures"* (NIV).

The Trap of Debt

Be aware that the enemy may give you curses disguised as blessings in order to rob you of your inheritance. For example, perhaps you have received a credit card offer that says you have been preapproved for a $5,000 credit limit. Do not jump up and down and praise God! That card is not a blessing from Him. Credit is pure debt, and a river cannot flow from a place of indebtedness. A river in debt is just a desert.

When people use a credit card to purchase nonessentials and become financially burdened because they can't pay off the card, it means that the card is not from God. It is a temptation from the enemy.

The hidden clauses and fine print in contracts can come back to bite the one who buys into the façade. For instance, are the frequent credit card offers we get in the mail really free money? Do they bring instant relief when the bills are due? They may seem that way, until the credit card bill arrives with exorbitant interest tacked on. Soon, the rising credit card bills become more of an issue than the original problem.

The Poverty Mind-set

A man I know was complaining about losing both his car and house. Even though he was a very influential leader, he spoke from a mind-set of poverty. We discussed this point in chapter 1, but I can't emphasize it enough: you must live with a mind-set of prosperity, not poverty. Remember, *"death and life are in the power of the tongue"* (Proverbs 18:21).

Never allow such negative words to come out of your mouth. Instead, make plans to pay off your mortgage and your car. Prepare to receive more and more, far beyond anything you have ever received. Believe that you will have more than enough. Map out what you'll do with the blessings of God when they arrive.

If you need to break the spirit of poverty, pray this prayer aloud:

Father, in the name of Jesus, I renounce and break off the spirit of poverty. In Jesus' name, I declare that I no longer walk in poverty, and that I am going to walk in prosperity, according to Your Word. I will walk in prosperity, not only in my finances, but in every area of my life.

Father, I have the mind of Christ, not a poverty mind-set. All negative thinking is gone, in Jesus' name. Any fear is gone, in Jesus' name. I will limit the time I spend watching the news and listening to naysayers. I will no longer allow the opinions of man to direct me. Instead, I will turn to Your Word for divine direction. I am blessed to be a blessing to others, in Jesus' name. Amen!

Vague Prayers

A little boy was playing with his brother when he fell and bumped his head. His mother put her hand on his shoulder and began to pray, but he took her hand, moved it to his head, and said, "No, Mommy, my shoulder doesn't hurt; my head hurts." Even a four-year-old understood that his mom needed to put her hand in the right place when she prayed.

> **When you pray for your finances, be specific. God is ready to pour out His blessings to meet your needs, but you have to articulate what they are!**

When you pray for your finances, be specific. Like the boy told his mother, ask God to put His hand where it hurts. He is ready to pour out His blessings to meet your needs, but you have to articulate what they are! *"You do not have because you do not ask"* (James 4:2). Even though God knows our needs, He wants us to express them.

Do not stop with, "Father, bless my finances!"

Instead, say, "Father, I declare that I have more than enough money in my account to meet all my needs! Father, I am so glad I can give You more than just 10 percent of my income. Father, I can freely give whatever, whenever, and wherever You tell me to give. I can be a radical giver. I am a cheerful giver. Thank You for all Your blessings."

Consider this specific prayer of Jabez from the book of 1 Chronicles:

> *And Jabez called on the God of Israel saying, "Oh, that You would bless me indeed, and enlarge my territory, that Your hand would be with me, and that You would keep me from evil, that I may not cause pain!"* (1 Chronicles 4:10)

How did God respond? *"So God granted him what he requested"* (verse 10). He heard the particulars of Jabez's prayer, and He granted them!

Laying Claim through Prayer for Specific Needs

I want you to be financially healthy. I want you to be able to give freely to further God's work. I want the windows of heaven to open wide so that your inheritance of abundant prosperity may overwhelm you in every area of your life.

Now that we have discussed the keys to breakthrough in your finances, I am going to lead you in prayer in regard to specific situations. If a situation pertains to you, pray about it by name. Be specific. All the hindering forces in your life must go at your command! You are going to commission jobs and promotions, break the spirit of poverty, and declare pay raises, bonuses, and donations to support what God has given you to do. If hindering forces have stopped the flow of finances

Do you need physical healing? Call it by name. Could you use more finances? Say exactly what your need is.

in your life, be specific when you pray against them, naming your need. Do you need physical healing? Call it by name. Could you use more finances? Say exactly what your need is.

I will start by agreeing with you in prayer. "Father, I agree with Your will for this dear reader's life, and I come against any hindering spirits that have been blocking the full release of Your blessings, in Jesus' name. Amen."

Now it's your turn! Roll up your sleeves and put on your fighting gloves. When you come to a prayer that fits your specific need, pray it aloud. That way, you will see the words, read the words, and hear the words—a threefold reinforcement.

If someone owes you money...

"Father, I thank You in Jesus' name that any money owed to me will be restored quickly. Bless (*insert name*), Father, so that he or she may fulfill this commitment. In the name of Jesus, I ask You to move in the heart of my debtor to pay me the money I am owed so that I may use it to bless others. In Jesus' name, amen."

If you work in sales with a commission...

"Father, You know that I work on a commission basis. I command any forces that would hinder my success to be gone, in Jesus' name. I speak supernatural increase for my sales, in Jesus' name. Amen."

If you desire an increase in pay and bonuses...

"Father, I believe You want to bless and prosper me, so, whether I have been promised a pay raise or not, I speak a pay raise into my finances. I speak bonuses into my life, in Jesus' name. Amen."

If you desire or need a different job...

"Father, I thank You for the job you have planned for me. I thank You for the job that is coming in the near future that will far exceed any hope, dream, or desire I have, in Jesus' name. Amen."

If you need donations or outside income to support your ministry...

"Father, I command any forces that are hindering church members or ministry partners from giving generously to You and Your work to be gone, in Jesus' name. Father, I thank You that the support they have pledged will come in supernaturally, in Jesus' name. Amen."

If you need a new home or want your home paid off this year...

"Father, I thank You for the home coming to me in the near future, in Jesus' name."

"Father, in the name of Jesus, I thank You that my home mortgage is supernaturally paid off. Amen."

If you need a new car or your existing vehicle requires repairs...

"Father, I need a new car. Thank You for supernaturally supplying enough money and/or discounts for me to pay for it in full, in Jesus' name. Amen."

"Father, I have a bill for car repairs that I must pay off. Thank You for providing what is needed to pay this bill in full, in Jesus' name. Amen."

If you have credit card debt...

"Father, You know that I have credit card debt. But I thank You that all the debt will be paid off quickly. Thank You for helping me to supernaturally pay off my debt, as well as for helping me to change my habits so that I never fall into debt again, in Jesus' name. Amen."

If you (or someone you know) desire to be pregnant...

"Father, I want to be pregnant/I have a friend or family member who is having trouble getting pregnant. I command any hindering forces to be gone, in Jesus' name. I command the fallopian tubes and uterus to be open and receptive to conception and for an increase in sperm, in Jesus' name. Amen." (I prayed this prayer for my daughter, and she got pregnant four days later!)

If you desire a godly spouse...

"Father, I thank You that the spouse You have selected for me is coming to me. Thank You that You have been preparing me for him/her. I want to be a blessing to my future spouse, who is already on the way into my life. Thank You, Father, in Jesus' name. Amen."

If you are married to an unsaved spouse...

"Father, I thank You for removing any hindering forces that are preventing my spouse from coming to salvation. I thank You for the salvation of my spouse, in Jesus' name. Amen."

If you have unsaved children...

"Father, I command the hindering forces that are keeping my children from coming to You to be gone. I claim Isaiah 49:25, in which You have promised to save my children. Thank You for Acts 16:31: *'Believe on the Lord Jesus Christ, and you will be saved, you and your household.'* No more hindrances! No more delays, in Jesus' name. Amen."

If you and your spouse struggle to give each other your best...

"Father, I pray that I would become the man/woman of God that my spouse deserves, that I will be the husband/wife You want me to be for him/her, in Jesus' name. Amen."

Well done! What you have just prayed has released the power of God to change your life and the lives of others.

Now, repeat the following sentence a number of times: "I am blessed to be a blessing!" You are breaking the spirit of poverty as you repeat that phrase over and over. Say it louder and louder: "I am blessed to be a blessing! I am blessed to be a blessing! I am blessed to be a blessing!"

Chapter 9

Avoiding Financial Potholes

*We desire that each one of you show the same dili-
gence to the full assurance of hope until the end,
that you do not become sluggish, but imitate those
who through faith and patience inherit the promises.*
—Hebrews 6:11–12

To summarize the principles we have discussed, I would like to share with you a hypothetical anecdote that illustrates a journey common to many of us. As you read, pay attention to the protagonist and the "potholes" he falls into along the way, taking note of any that particularly resonate with you. At the conclusion of the story, we will put into practice some of the methods we have discussed, contradicting the devil's lies and the world's opinions with the truth of God's Word.

The Journey

As a young boy sitting in a hardwood pew in a denominational church, he felt but could not identify the stirring of the Holy Spirit in his belly. He would watch the faithful take their territorial seats, listen, and smile as the Sunday ritual ran its predictable course. Offering time and the passing of the plates were part of the ritual. The curious young boy glanced at the plate as it passed by, and, on occasion, he deposited a contribution of his own. He did this sparingly, though, because from what he saw as the plate passed, he assumed that God did not need much money to keep the big, beautiful church operating. In fact, it confirmed to him that God did not need anyone to give any money, because the church was open, clean, and beautiful every Sunday morning. The offering plate and the money that collected there did not seem to have any connection to the needs of the church, in the young boy's mind.

As he grew into a young man, he became quite industrious and kept an eye out for extra opportunities to make money and acquire worldly possessions. As he earned more money and took advantage of profitable investment opportunities, the acquisition of material goods became the main focus of his life.

Opportunities seemed to appear everywhere he looked. With a knack for purchasing items to sell for more than they cost him, he was always looking for easy ways to make a profit. He subscribed to the worldly maxim "The bigger, the better," and he found great success and satisfaction in acquiring and accumulating more and more, which, to him, equated to a job well done.

Feeding the need to get more and do more, he started a new business venture and moved for the first time from out-of-pocket spending to reliance on the world's system of credit through a loan. Little had he anticipated how quickly the cycle of debt would become the master and director of his business. For the first time, he realized that the ability to acquire and keep came at a price called interest.

A unique positioning and a broad scope of merchandise offered him the luxury of market domination in his area. He became the go-to guy and reaped the financial rewards of a successful business. The success caused a snowball effect. The more product he sold, the more capital he needed to buy additional product while still paying off his debt. The only way to keep up was by using the world's system: going into greater debt to purchase more items to sell. Would-be business partners would approach him on a regular basis, trying to get in on the action, asking for a piece of the pie. The enormous success of his startup business in its first year, along with his six-figure income, fueled his belief that his own abilities and talents alone had made it happen.

It was no secret to this self-made man that God had taken a backseat on his journey to the top. When a close friend invited him to a service at a local church, he accepted. In fact, he found himself returning to church every Sunday for the next few weeks, as his need for a divine encounter became more and more evident. Yes, he was highly successful in the marketplace and had credit to purchase above and beyond his heart's desires, but some-

For the first time, he realized that church attendance does not constitute a personal relationship with God.

thing was missing. The people at church had something he didn't—something his money could not buy. They had a personal relationship with God, and it was evident in their attitudes, their words, and their actions. He had attended church for many years, but now, for the first time, he realized that church attendance does not constitute a personal relationship with God. *All this time, I've known about God*, he thought, *but I don't really know Him.*

Hearing a sermon that spoke to his heart, he made an awkward journey down the aisle to the front of the church and committed his life to the Lord. In his earlier years, he'd thought he was saved, but now, having confessed Jesus as his Lord and Savior, he knew he was heaven bound. He'd finally crossed over from knowing about God to knowing Him, and this transition began a season of reflection and change.

He became more involved in the church and, as he did so, was given the opportunity to tithe and give money toward charitable works. The question from his youth came up again: "Does God really need my money?" Tithing did not add up in a natural way as his view of the world and the marketplace did. His impression of tithing, up until this point in his life, had led him to see it as an unfruitful practice, a waste of money. To him, it still made more sense to use his money to invest, buy, and sell for the purpose of personal gain. He fell back to relying on his own abilities and desires!

Several years passed, and his business continued to grow and prosper. However, increasing debt demanded more and more of his attention. He still attended church, where the people appeared to be content, even though they had nowhere near the riches that he had. The realization was difficult for him to understand, for, to him, less money meant less happiness. It seemed to him that God did not want His children to have both happiness and abundant finances.

He knew that church projects and missions trips require funding. He could acknowledge that spreading the gospel and raising a Christian family demanded finances, just as owning and operating his business did. Then, why did he find it so hard to give money to the church? Maybe it was God's plan for His people to just get by, because where were the blessings and abundance? Where was God's supernatural provision? Was it entirely bad to have wealth and costly possessions?

Having a personal relationship with the Lord satisfied him in a new, exciting way, however. His journey had taken God from the backseat to the front seat of his life, or so he thought. With a burning desire to know more about God, he came to view church as a way of life, not just a place to go for something to do. The businessman continued his quest to amass wealth, though, and he did so by dividing his material pursuits and his spiritual practices into two different worlds. To him, faith and finances were incompatible. He believed that the two had no connection whatsoever in the natural, and certainly not in the spirit realm.

In his dichotomous mind-set, it was perfectly acceptable to pray for the church—its members, its missions, and even its finances. Yet he never would have considered praying for his personal finances or business.

This system of separating his spiritual life from his professional/business life seemed to work just fine. Still, in the back of his mind, he wondered if he was experiencing "life to the fullest," as God intended him to. (See John 10:10.)

The businessman journeyed over many peaks and through many valleys that might have caused a weaker person to give up. Yet God fanned a small ember within this man that ignited the desire for a new journey with Him as the pilot of his life. Finally, the businessman was ready to step down and assume the position of copilot. This change entailed a geographic move, which he obediently undertook, keeping in mind the words of Jesus in Luke 14:33: *"Whoever of you does not forsake all that he has cannot be My disciple."*

The man found a new church where the Spirit-filled pastor taught a biblical view of abundance. And he received the teaching like a dried-out sponge in a rainstorm. Where had this pastor discovered that it was acceptable for Christians to have abundant finances? The businessman soon developed an insatiable appetite for the Bible's teachings on finances.

After more instruction, more teaching, more divine relationships, and more prayer, he changed his attitude from "I can do it" to "God will do it." He finally came to realize that God knew his every need and desire before he became aware of it or prayed about it.

He finally came to realize that God knew his every need and desire before he became aware of it or prayed about it.

Soon, the blessings of God began to overtake him every day. He caught a glimpse of things to come and now seeks God for additional revelation and knowledge in every area of his life.

When he started listening to the Spirit-filled pastor at his new church, he received a revelation of Deuteronomy 1:11—*"May the LORD God of your fathers make you a thousand times more numerous than you are, and bless you as He has promised you!"*—that confirmed he was hearing God's voice and following His direction. With the knowledge that God wanted to make him a thousand times greater in every area of his life, the businessman submitted to His vision. Because of his obedience, God led him to a place where he could grow and flourish in a ministry chosen for such a time as this.

Set Free by the Truth

The man in this story was highly successful, in the world's eyes, yet he could not enjoy the priceless blessing of a relationship with God until he had cleared up several major misconceptions that were keeping him stuck in "potholes" along the road to spiritual maturity.

Let's apply what we've discussed as we identify each one of these misconceptions and then look at a Scripture that tells the truth about the situation. This will enable us to recognize misconceptions in our own lives, which we can then correct with the truth, in fulfillment of John 8:32: *"And you shall know the truth, and the truth shall make you free."*

Misconception #1: "The church does not need my money."

"Will a man rob God? Yet you have robbed Me! But you say, 'In what way have we robbed You?' In tithes and offerings. You are cursed with a curse, for you have robbed Me, even this whole nation. Bring all the tithes into the storehouse, that there may be food in My house, and try Me now in this," says the LORD of hosts, "if I will not open for you the windows of heaven and pour out for you such blessing that there will not be room enough to receive it. And I will rebuke the devourer for your sakes, so that he will not destroy the fruit of your ground, nor shall the vine fail to bear fruit for you in the field," says the LORD of hosts. (Malachi 3:8–11)

Misconception #2: "Succeeding in business and accumulating wealth brings the ultimate fulfillment in life."

[Jesus said,] *"The ground of a certain rich man yielded plentifully. And he thought within himself, saying, 'What shall I do, since I have no room to store my crops?' So he said, 'I will do this: I will pull down my barns and build greater, and there I will store all my crops and my goods. And I will say to my soul, "Soul, you have many goods laid up for many years; take your ease; eat, drink, and be merry."' But God said to him, 'Fool! This night your soul will be required of you; then whose will those things be which you have provided?' So is he who lays up treasure for himself, and is not rich toward God....Sell what you have and give alms; provide yourselves money bags which do not grow old, a treasure in the heavens that does not fail, where no thief approaches nor moth destroys. For where your treasure is, there your heart will be also."* (Luke 12:16–21, 33–34)

Command those who are rich in this present age not to be haughty, nor to trust in uncertain riches but in the living God, who gives us richly all things to enjoy. Let them do good, that they be rich in good works, ready to give, willing to share, storing up for themselves a good foundation for the time to come, that they may lay hold on eternal life. (1 Timothy 6:17–19)

Misconception #3: "Man gets the credit for the wealth he earns."

*And you shall remember the L*ORD *your God, for it is He who gives you power to get wealth.*
(Deuteronomy 8:18)

What are you so puffed up about? What do you have that God hasn't given you? And if all you have is from God, why act as though you are so great, and as though you have accomplished something on your own? (1 Corinthians 4:7 TLB)

Misconception #4: "God provides just enough for His children, nothing more."

Let the LORD be magnified, who has pleasure in the prosperity of His servant. (Psalm 35:27)

You will be made rich in every way so that you can be generous on every occasion, and through us your generosity will result in thanksgiving to God. (2 Corinthians 9:11 NIV)

Possess Your Promised Land

Starting today, you will be held to a higher level of accountability with your finances because of what you have learned of God's ways in this book. When you apply God's wisdom and instructions to your finances, His miracle blessings will break into your life. Your body will be healed. Your finances will improve. Blessings of all kinds will rain down upon you. God will resurrect some of the money that you lost over time. People who have owed you money for years will start paying you what they owe, which will also allow there to be reconciliation and restoration in your relationships.

The blessings of God will follow you and overtake you wherever you go. God knows exactly where you are at all times, and He will send blessings to you, no matter where you are in the world. He also has a sense of humor and may bless you in the most surprising ways. Again, you are blessed to be a blessing, not to hoard. When you give, it will be returned to you, and to a greater degree.

When you have been praying for a specific need and you receive an answer, always thank God for His gracious provision. Remember, He is the lover of your soul, your Abba Father, Jehovah Jireh—the God who provides. You are His child, and *"every good gift and every perfect gift is from...the Father"* (James 1:17).

Do not give up on your dreams and visions. Fulfill the destiny God has for you. If you take this revelation and live by it, you will experience all of the miracles God has in store. He is taking you from recession to possession!

Chapter 10

Personal Testimonies

Oh, give thanks to the LORD, for He is good! For His mercy endures forever....Oh, that men would give thanks to the LORD for His goodness, and for His wonderful works to the children of men! For He satisfies the longing soul, and fills the hungry soul with goodness.
—Psalm 107:1, 8–9

God delights in the prosperity of His servants. As proof, we receive testimonies about financial miracles at our ministry on a daily basis! Miracle babies are being born, miracle healings are happening, and miracle finances are being showered upon the people of God. Some days, it is hard to keep up with them all! I have chosen to include a few testimonies here, so that your faith and belief may be strengthened. Remember, these blessings are coming to everyday people from all walks of life around the world.

As you read about the miracles of provision in others' lives, I encourage you to feel the excitement coming through their words, let your faith grow, and believe for your own miracles. Don't forget to write me about the supernatural provision God brings to your home and family.

A young woman listened to my teachings on supernatural provision. Within a short time, she learned that a $1,500 debt that she had owed had been totally forgiven. Later, she was summoned to her boss's office. The company had been laying off employees for the past few months, and she thought she was next. Instead of being fired, she received a promotion and a raise in pay!

After sitting in one of my services and praying that someone who owed her money for a job she had done would pay her, a woman received a phone call on her way home from church. Her husband called to tell her a $13,000 check had arrived to pay off a fifteen-year-old debt!

A couple came from Mesa, Arizona, to a conference on finances I was holding in Albuquerque, New Mexico. When they got home, the babysitter they had hired to watch their five children refused to accept the $200 they wanted to pay her.

Other miracles followed. They were closing on a house in the near future, and they had money in their safe in preparation for that day. As they got ready for the closing, they went to the safe to double-check the amount they had so carefully saved. There was $2,700 more than what their records showed! They were so excited because of what God had done. A few days later, they counted their money again to be sure they had totaled it accurately. This time, the amount was

$3,200 more. They called me immediately, and we rejoiced together at God's kindness toward them.

Some people have had money show up unexpectedly in their bank accounts. They were surprised and questioned the bank. Instead of trying to logically figure out what happened and why, they learned to say "Thank You, Jesus!" and gratefully accepted the unexpected blessings.

"During one of your services in Ohio, you mentioned that we would be hearing about full-ride college scholarships. About a month and a half ago, my married son received a call from a university asking if he was interested in getting his master's degree. A year before, he had applied for a scholarship but had been denied. This caller asked if he was still interested. They wanted to give him a second chance. He received a full-ride scholarship! I know beyond a shadow of doubt that it was God! This scholarship will be worth $50,000 to $60,000. Praise God!"

A church I was ministering in gave a small amount in the offering. At the time, it was all they could afford. A complete stranger walked in and seeded $1,000 into the church.

A woman was praying for her own home. She backed up her faith by seeding specifically for a home. The city of Lincoln, Nebraska, gives away a new home every year. They pass out fifteen keys, and the person holding the right key gets a home free of charge. She received the winning key and now lives in a beautiful home, totally debt-free.

Several years ago, a coworker of my daughter Melody's was going through a divorce. This woman had a teenage daughter, as well as two young children. In a panic, she called Melody and said, "I don't know what to do. They are going to shut off my power on Friday. I don't have $250 to pay the bill or the reconnect fee after they turn it off. I'm just so upset."

Melody prayed with her and said, "God knows what you need and when you need it. We just need Him to get someone to move on your behalf." Friday was fast approaching, and on Thursday night, she called to check on her friend. Her friend had e-mailed several people, letting them know of the problem at hand. Only one had responded—and said that helping her would not be possible.

Melody told her, "God put it on my heart to help you." She gave her the $250 to keep the electricity turned on. Her friend was very hesitant to accept the money, but, knowing it was coming down to the last minute, she swallowed her pride and received.

In the natural, this seems like Melody just happened to be a good person concerned for her friend's children. You could say that she just chose to do it because she was being nice or doing "the Christian thing." Actually, more was going on than Melody's friend realized. My daughter was planting a seed in obedience to God, and He would honor her faithfulness.

Four days after Melody helped her friend with the electric bill, one of her clients tipped her $250 for the work she had done for his family. The couple had no idea why they were tipping so generously. It was truly God moving on their heart to bless her.

It was awesome to hear about Melody's explanation to this couple as to why God had told them to give so much.

She could have said, "This is too much. I can't receive this." Instead, she was able to explain to them that their gift was how God had honored His word to her.

As we discussed in chapter 5, it's a blessing to partner with ministries that are doing God's work. The following are the testimonies of some of our partners.

"Since becoming a partner with Joan Hunter Ministries, I have seen my finances blessed beyond measure. I recently received a promotion. I was given more territory (the only woman ever to get any territory in this company) and a substantial raise plus bonuses."

"I became a partner a few years ago and have traveled with Joan Hunter Ministries as often as I can. I love ministering with Joan and being a part of the team. This year, I received a promotion (with a pay raise) and a bonus plan (84 bonuses a year), in addition to permission to travel with the ministry whenever I need to."

"I believed to get out of debt this year. I seeded in Joan Hunter Ministries, and within two weeks, I was out of debt."

"I was in debt and didn't know how to get out. I came to a conference, where I repented and planted my seed. Did God ever bless that seed! I am completely out of debt. Thank You, Jesus!"

"My husband gave me $40 to give in the offering as I left for church. Offering time came, and I gave the $40, plus $12 I had in my pocket. It was all I had. Before the service was over, I received a call from my husband, stating that I had received a bonus of over 100 times what I just seeded in the offering that night."

"I gave money toward an offering on Monday night. Then, on Tuesday, I was going to the car to head to a service when my neighbor came running outside and gave me an envelope. On my way to the service, I opened the envelope. It was full of $20 bills."

"I believed God for money for some new clothes I needed for my new job. I seeded for all my needs to be met. The next week, I received a check and a note specifically saying I was to use the money for clothes. God cares about everything that concerns us."

"I prayed the hindering forces off of my son and his schoolwork. He was later chosen as best in the class to go before the whole school."

"My son wanted to get into a particular preparatory school that had turned him down several times. We listened to your teaching CD and applied what it said, and, two hours later on a *Saturday*, the school called to tell him he had been accepted."

"We are in the real estate business and hadn't closed on anything in four months. We got your teaching CD and prayed the prayers. The next week, we had five closings and more the following week. We are scheduling a showing every two hours because God's windows of heaven have opened up over our business."

"I am working around my house, confessing, 'I am blessed to be a blessing!' And God's blessings are pouring in."

"I just started a new job at a bank. My responsibility is to bring in new clients. After I had listened to the teaching, six new clients brought in over a million dollars to the bank in a time when no new accounts were being opened."

"I had put a deposit down for a trip that I had to cancel. After numerous attempts to get a refund, I applied what was on your CD. They called me the next week and have returned some of the money. The rest is coming next month! Praise God!"

"We are in the commercial real estate business and have had many deals fall through. We spoke over each of them with the revelation of your teachings on supernatural financial provision. These 'dead' deals have been resurrected and are coming through. Thank you for sharing your revelation."

"Someone owed me money for over six years. After I listened to your teaching on finances, I received a phone call a week later, and that person paid me some of the money."

"I needed a new truck, and I was believing for a new job that requires special training. I listened to your CD and wrote down my goals and all that I am trusting God to provide. The next day, a miracle truck came across my path. It is now mine! Paid for in full! Also, the next day, the school opened up for me to get certified for my new job."

"I got back more from the IRS this year than I made in 2000. I gave into the kingdom more than two times what I made in 2000. The more I give, the more I receive. God can trust me with His increase. This is not bragging on me; it is bragging on Him!"

We gave a sacrificial gift of $5 in your service last week. Before we left the meeting, God told someone to give us a check for $500—the exact amount we were believing for! Thank You, Jesus."

"I needed to have my truck repaired. The estimate from the shop was $700. I walked around my house, saying, 'I am blessed to be a blessing!' When I went to pick up my vehicle, the total read $350. When I questioned the repairman about the difference, he said, 'Ma'am, someone just came in and paid half the bill!' Thank You, Jesus!"

"I had a lawsuit pending regarding a large settlement. This situation was holding up payment of my money. I listened to your CD on *Supernatural Provision* and prayed the prayers. The lawsuit was dropped the next morning. Thank You, Jesus!"

"I needed my car repaired while I was on vacation. It was going to cost $450, which was not in my budget. When I went to pick up the car, the bill had already been paid. Thank You, Jesus!"

"My daughter was having a hard time getting pregnant after two and a half years of trying. I got your CD on finances and prayed the prayer regarding hindrances that were keeping her from getting pregnant. She got pregnant that week! Thank You, Jesus."

"After hearing you speak on finances, I feel like I can hope again. Your teachings have been such a blessing. I feel so good to have my hope renewed and believe that prosperity is on its way!"

A couple was believing to get out of debt quickly. A man walked up to them at church and gave them a check for a thousand dollars as he said, "God told me to give you this!"

"Someone sent me $1,000 for the Fourth of July! A blessing for freedom!"

"I am buying my first house. The price is 33 percent off the appraised value! Thank You, Jesus!"

"I am seeding, and even my children are getting blessed financially!"

"I applied for a job, along with 50 other applicants. I was the only one called back for a second interview. I got the job!"

"We are continuing our study of *Supernatural Provision* and trying to get in sync with the practice of scriptural giving. This month, we sowed $111.11 into your ministry. This week, the Lord removed a debt of $11,500.00 that we had been carrying. Totally God! We are in awe! Glory to God and to Him only!"

"We are currently shopping for a new home to move into—one that is ours. I now tell everyone I talk to about *Supernatural Provision*—the message is life altering! Don't just listen to it. You have to do what it says! If you do, I guarantee that it will change your life!"

"I was a single mom for over five years. We had a time of financial difficulty, as you might expect. My ex-husband abandoned us and paid no child support. My son and I had all of our basic needs met, according to the Word of the Lord, but I was praying for more.

"I heard Joan talking about *Supernatural Provision* in January 2008. I listened to her teaching CD at least five times driving back and forth to work. I kept hearing about all the financial breakthroughs and miracles that were happening to other people, and, to be honest, I was quite frustrated.

I went to the Lord in prayer one day and cried out, saying, 'Lord! I keep hearing about all these miracles happening for other people. Why aren't they happening for me?' The Lord told me, 'That's because you've only been listening to the CD. You haven't done what it says.'

"After hearing that, I listened to the CD once more, but, this time, I sat down at my dining room table, and I did what Joan said. I made the lists, said the prayers, and called in those things Joan declared that God says we can have.

"Sure enough, right after that, I got engaged and married a short time later to a wonderful man who is also a great father. He owns a two-story house in a very nice area of Houston and treats me really well."

"In 2009, after hearing the teaching on *Supernatural Provision*, I prayed the prayer of repentance for all of my past sins in the area of finances—for any foolish spending, for any time I hadn't tithed, and for any time I hadn't given an offering when God had spoken to my heart to do so.

"My daughter graduated from college in December 2009 as a teacher and started looking for a job—slowly at first but full steam ahead beginning in March 2010. She went to job fairs, looked online regularly, and sent her resume to almost every school district within a 50-mile radius around the Houston area. No results!

"Her heart's desire was to work at the school where she had completed her internship, but there were no openings. Finally, in the month when school would begin for the 2010–2011 school year, a position opened at that school. She immediately applied in person. When she submitted her application and resume, she was told that the position had been filled. Feeling disappointed and discouraged, she told me about ten days before school was to start that she was just going to start looking for a job she was qualified for outside of the teaching profession.

"She had heard about a position at an orphanage and said she planned to apply the next day. The job sounded good.

"Before she went to bed that night, I said, 'Let's pray before you go.' We prayed the prayer from Joan's financial teaching concerning hindering spirits, and we commanded all hindering spirits, voices, or forces that were hindering her from getting the job God had ordained for her to go, in Jesus' name!

"We called forth the job God had chosen for her, in Jesus' name. Amazingly—thank You, Jesus—the next day around lunchtime, she got a call to come in to interview for the teaching job at the school where she had done her internship—the job she had previously been told was already filled.

Right now, God wants you to get into alignment with the Word so that He can open the windows of heaven and pour out His blessings on you.

"She was hired and started working the very next day, attending meetings and setting up her third-grade classroom just the way she wanted it! God truly gave her the desires of her heart, approximately twelve hours after we had prayed against hindering spirits! What a mighty God we serve!"

A woman was depending on child support from her ex-husband. When he was arrested and imprisoned, all support stopped. In order to feed her children, she used credit cards to purchase food. One day, someone contacted her and told her he wanted to pay off her credit cards. She was prepared to receive God's blessings. God supplied over and abundantly to meet her needs.

What Is Your Testimony?

God wants to pour out the blessings of heaven in every area of your life, as well. Are you ready? Are you prepared to sow? Are you prepared to receive? Are your barns built and ready to receive His overwhelming harvest of blessings? Perhaps you don't want a barn. Do you have a savings account ready and waiting?

Right now, God wants you to get into alignment with the Word so that He can open the windows of heaven and pour out His blessings on you. Are you going to open your umbrella to protect yourself from those blessings? I doubt it. You will turn that umbrella upside down and catch everything God wants to send your way.

Do not look to the natural for your income. God is your Provider, and He will supernaturally provide all you need.

Here is something fun you can do: Add up everything you owe. Why? To make you feel bad? No! You never know; someone might walk up to you and say, "How much do you owe? I want to write a check right now to pay off all your debts!" Could you answer him? Be prepared. Plan on it happening to you! Include your mortgage, your car loan, and your credit card liabilities. Expect it!

When you go to the mailbox, say, "Father, I am excited about what You are going to send."

If there is something in your mailbox, say, "Praise God!"

If there isn't anything, say, "Not today," or "Not yet, but it is coming." Don't be negative. Speak positive words in faith, and trust God to provide. He will get it to you if He can get it through you!

This is my prayer on your behalf:

Father, thank You for Your Word. Thank You for freely giving us Your keys to success in this life. Thank You for opening our eyes and hearts to understand Your instruction.

Father, in response to their obedience to Your Word, bless those who read this book by giving them creativity and diligence to make money to seed into Your kingdom.

Father, give them wisdom on how to increase what they already have and wisdom on how to spend the finances with which You have blessed them. We will all rejoice and praise You for Your faithfulness to always keep Your promises. Thank You, Father, in Jesus' name. Amen.

Conclusion

God's Greatest Provision

And therefore the Lord [earnestly] waits [expecting, looking, and longing] to be gracious to you; and therefore He lifts Himself up, that He may have mercy on you and show loving-kindness to you. For the Lord is a God of justice. Blessed (happy, fortunate, to be envied) are all those who [earnestly] wait for Him, who expect and look and long for Him [for His victory, His favor, His love, His peace, His joy, and His matchless, unbroken companionship]!
—Isaiah 30:18 (AMP)

I cannot teach on God's wondrous blessings without discussing His most precious gift to mankind. Without this gift, most of what you have been studying throughout this book would not be possible. You could not receive His blessings. You would not understand them. You could not be part of the body of Christ. Instead, you would be on your way to destruction.

God sent His Son Jesus to die in your place so that you could be reconciled to Him. No amount of wealth, finances, or riches can equal the value of the precious gift of Jesus Christ. Because of His substitutionary death, you received your ultimate inheritance—eternal, abundant life in Him. You are not waiting to receive it at some future date; you have it! However, you have to accept it, and you have to claim it.

The most precious gift God freely shares with you is the most valuable blessing ever bestowed. Nothing can surpass or equal the treasure that has been given to you. Each person has to simply accept, believe, and receive.

> **All the financial prosperity in the world will not satisfy you unless your soul is "prospering." Everything depends on putting Jesus Christ on the throne of your life and living to serve Him first.**

Through Jesus, you have everything. You have the right to ask God the Father for what you need, the right to pray in Jesus' name, and the right to eternal life. The sacrificial blood of Jesus gives you the freedom to live in and enjoy all of God's creation. You win the big prize, you can have it all! Jesus lives within you. He saved you. He teaches you. He is everything to you. Nothing can surpass the value of Jesus—God's gift to the world, to you.

I love 3 John 2: *"Beloved, I pray that you may prosper in all things and be in health, just as your soul prospers."* All the financial prosperity in the world will not satisfy you unless your soul is "prospering." Everything depends on putting Jesus Christ on the throne of your life and living to serve Him first.

For God so loved the world that He gave His only begotten Son, that whoever believes in Him should not perish but have everlasting life. (John 3:16)

In order to be on the winning side, you must believe in Jesus and be saved. This is the greatest blessing of all. Now is a great opportunity to rededicate your life to God or even come to the Lord for the first time.

Say this aloud:

Father, I have sinned. I repent of my sin. Take this sin from me and place it on the cross of Jesus Christ, never to be held against me again. Jesus, I ask You to come into my life and be the Lord of my life. Not just my Savior, but also the Lord of my life.

Father, through Your Holy Spirit, lead me and guide me into all You have for me to do. I thank You that, from this day forward, my steps are ordered by You.

Father, I thank You for not only saving me, in Jesus' name, but also for supernaturally prospering me in every area of my life—body, mind, soul, spirit, and finances. Amen.

You now have the treasure of the world within your heart. You have the mind of Christ. You have all the wealth of your Father at your disposal. You are a joint heir with Jesus of everything the Father can give you. His Spirit is within you, and you have eternal life. (See Romans 8:14–18.)

As I come to the close of this book, I want to challenge you to put to use what you have learned within these pages. Don't read them and then file the book in your bookcase to collect dust. Use God's principles to change your life.

When the enemy tells you that depression or recession is knocking on your front door, send Jesus to answer it. When He opens the door, I guarantee the enemy and all his lies will run in the other direction.

As you stand strong in faith for what God has planned for you, miracles will occur regularly. Share those miracles with everyone else. Encourage others to believe in His Word also. Stay around positive Christian believers who will stand with you in agreement for more miracles.

Choose to live by God's economy and enjoy His bountiful blessings!

Believe. Give. Share. Receive. Plant. Harvest. Be blessed! Praise Him!

You can now add to your "Blessing List." You have received:

- God's Holy Spirit within you
- Eternal life
- New earthly life
- A new heart
- The mind of Christ
- Divine protection
- Freedom
- Peace
- Love
- Joy

You are heaven bound. See you there!

About the Author

At the tender age of twelve, Joan Hunter committed her life to Christ and began faithfully serving in ministry alongside her parents, Charles and Frances Hunter. Together, they traveled around the globe conducting Healing Explosions and Healing Schools.

Joan is an anointed healing evangelist, a dynamic teacher, and a best-selling author. She is the founder and president of Joan Hunter Ministries, Hearts 4 Him, and 4 Corners Foundation, and she is also the president of Hunter Ministries. Joan's television appearances have been broadcast around the world on World Harvest Network, Inspiration Network, Daystar, Faith TV, Cornerstone TV, The Church Channel, Total Christian Television, Christian Television Network, Watchmen Broadcasting, and God TV. Joan has also been the featured guest on many national television and radio shows, including Sid Roth's *It's Supernatural!*, *It's a New Day*, *The Miracle Channel*, *The Patricia King Show*, and many others.

Together, Joan and her powerful international healing ministry have ministered in miracle services and conducted healing schools throughout numerous countries in a world characterized by brokenness and pain. Having emerged victorious through tragic circumstances, impossible obstacles, and immeasurable devastation, Joan shares her personal message of hope and restoration to the brokenhearted, deliverance and freedom to the bound, and healing and wholeness to the diseased. Her vision is to see the body of Christ live in freedom, happiness, wholeness, and financial wellness.

Joan lives with her husband, Kelley Murrell, in Pinehurst, Texas. Together, they have eight children—four daughters and four sons—and four grandchildren.